ENDORSEMENTS

I have adored Lisa as a friend and sister in Christ for years. As I began to read this book, it was like sitting with her and having a conversation. The simplicity in everyday life can teach us so much if we slow down to listen. Lisa passionately shares personal moments with vulnerability and sincerity, humor, and humility. Her stories remind me of the simplicity needed for a relationship with God. After each story, she offers thought-provoking questions that help the reader apply the teaching. This book journey is worth your time!

Angel Steele, Friend and Sister in Christ

Florida

This book is a helpful guide to our spiritual needs. Lisa's teachings are food for thought and a way to increase personal Jesus awareness as a reminder that HIS likeness is always there, just like Charlie, eager and willing to listen. It's a guide to understanding how the Spirit is waiting and ready to go if we just pick up the leash and walk with God. I'm drawn to books with catchy titles and interesting subject matter. I read for entertainment and to learn, to gain knowledge and insight. I enjoy colorful words and phrases that help illustrate the intended meaning. This book checks all the boxes. I'm confident this book will change how you approach your own spiritual relationship.

Jen Bonitz, Friend

Pennsylvania

Charlie, Me, and Thee gives a delightful glance into how the Almighty reveals His character in the simplest ways in the simplest of creatures. I found myself picturing the scenes of sweet Charlie where I could almost smell puppy breath. Lisa invites us into an authentic examination of self with honesty, guidance, and of course grace and humor. Anyone who has a furry family member will enjoy the sweet connection of seeing how unconditional love comes from our Heavenly Father through the companion of a friend who never utters a word but teaches us such valuable lessons on life. Lisa's whimsical personality shines through, inviting us into authenticity and an opportunity to take a deeper look at how God speaks, if only we will slow down to notice His still small voice in still small ways. If donkeys can talk and see angels (Numbers 22) then surely Charlie can help us see the movements of God, His inexhaustible love, and teach us "masters" a thing or two.

Kelly Willie, Award-winning author, singer/songwriter,
Spiritual Director, and founder of Kelly at The Well and Pairables
Freeland, Maryland

Charlie, Me, and Thee is a beautiful testament to a beautiful faith; sharing truth, grace, and inspiration through the antics of one precious pug and inviting us to explore where we meet God in our own lives.

Cara Achterberg, author of Another Good Dog:
One Family and Fifty Foster Dogs
Virginia

CHARLIE, ME, *and* THEE

Things My Dog Taught Me About
GOD

LISA WEIGARD

Charlie, Me, and Thee
Things My Dog Taught Me About God
Lisa Weigard

To contact the author: CharlieMeThee@gmail.com

Published by:

Mary Ethel

Mary Ethel Eckard
Frisco, Texas

Library of Congress Cataloging in Publication Data: 2022906610

ISBN (Print): 979-8-9857287-3-6
ISBN (E-book): 979-8-9857287-4-3

To Tim, Maya, and Cole.

You are so loved.

I pray you always stay close to God and find

Him, too, in unexpected places.

Keep your eyes open and your heart soft.

Xo

Lisa / Mom

And to Charlie.

I know you won't be with us forever.

I doubt you know how much I learned from you.

I will forever be grateful.

Xo

Mom

To God.

Thank you for being patient with me.

Your love is truly yummy.

Xo

Lisa

CONTENTS

FOREWORD

When I was asked to write this Foreword, I was immediately filled with great joy in being able to introduce you to one of the most spectacular people on the earth!

I met Lisa years ago as our daughters were the same age and involved in similar things at church. We also overlapped when we served in children's ministry for a brief season, but then lost general contact for several years. Don't get me wrong; social media helped us keep track of each other, but there was no intentional pressing into a friendship at that time. We just ran in different circles. But from my circle, I watched her come into her own and I was deeply inspired. I observed how her soul longed to see women find their own soul's value, worth, and ability to shine. To achieve this, she stepped into the adventure of starting a boutique. I went into her shop one Saturday to peek at all the exciting things unfolding.

Lisa is a risk-taker and I wanted to be one too! She inspires so naturally the desire to ignite the internal flame of walking in your God-given destiny! I could see she was figuring out her design and she was calling out to others. I was doing very much the same thing at that same time. Our circles were overlapping!

That day in the shop, with delight in my eyes, I said, "I've been watching you." She responded, with a twinkle in her eyes, "I've been watching you."

There was such a catch of breath in the atmosphere. Her *Morning Tea with Me* videos inspired and cheered so many, but for me, it was also an example of how to make a positive, regular impact of truth and light in such a dark, desperate world. The Lord used her to speak about what I could do with my own life and influence.

Lisa is just that kind of person. You won't be able to hang around her and not feel the wind of the Holy Spirit, the chasing love of the Father, and the tender hand of Jesus. She loves the Lord, and it is obvious! She not only loves the Lord, but she also obeys the Lord. The combination of that brings explosions of joy and breakthrough everywhere she goes!

A year or so after that encounter, we overlapped again and this time our circles merged a bit. She came to a workshop I was leading. Another time, we met for tea. It was then we got to the heart of things we were seeing in the earth and what we thought God wanted to do about it through us! Yes, *through* us! We were so excited. The overlap grew and grew. Lisa and me - we are called together for such a time as this, and we are saying "yes" to God and "yes" to the soul-deep relationship He is creating between us.

Now that we run together, we have seen things and gone on some intense and fruitful adventures together! Whether she is worshiping, studying the Word, praying, ministering, laughing, crying, contemplative or fiery, she exudes a steadfast and diligent pursuit of God, His plans for her, and the people she encounters. She fights for people and nations (she prays BIG) with gusto, stamina, and Holy Spirit inspiration. She is a mountain mover and darkness dispeller. She loves hard and fierce and has a grit about her that keeps her getting back up, battle after battle. She is good stuff! If you need prayer, you want to have Lisa pray! If you need to confess a struggle, you want to have Lisa listen. If you are down, she will help you stand. If you are believing for big things, Lisa will believe right alongside you.

What I love about Lisa the most is that she is a person of FAITH! Like real, Biblical faith. The raising the dead, knocking down Jericho walls, healing lepers, casting out all the wrong that doesn't belong kind-of faith. You know, the kind of faith that Jesus calls all His disciples to. Lisa walks around doing and saying the things Jesus said and did. It is awesome to watch and inspiring to the core! You can't be around her and not sense the expectancy of God's goodness that she carries. She is expecting God to intersect her life every moment, and the testimony of that kind of expectation is that He really does break through our everyday moments, big and small, important, or neutral, and in the most unusual ways at times, such as through a dog. In Lisa's case, it's through her dog, Charlie!

It is so like God to use an animal to get His message across! I mean, He has done it before (Numbers 22:21-39)! Reading through Lisa's journey of learning about God through the lens of Charlie is an endearing, inspiring, challenging, faith-digging, grand adventure you will be so blessed to take. As with all things Lisa, you will sense the nearness of God through these pages and the invitation to see more of His goodness. So grab some tea, take your time, cuddle up with this book, and let God reveal Himself to you through Lisa and Charlie.

Krystal Woods
www.seasonsinthevine.com

INTRODUCTION

I'm not particularly great with dogs. If I'm completely transparent, I feel like I'm constantly figuring things out and always learning in nearly all aspects of life. I'm mom to two fabulous young adults, Maya and Cole (21 and 19 at the time of writing), married to Tim (we'll soon celebrate 25 years), and I own a women's boutique called Soulshine Boutique in Shrewsbury, Pennsylvania. I have been a Christian my whole life, leveling up every day, and I am definitely better at living out this Christian journey than I was several years ago. I am an everyday, average gal that simply started to ponder.

My dog, Charlie, created enough of a break in my routine to thoughtfully consider the deeper things. These tiny ponders started to accumulate and, knowing how the busy life so often distracts and those lovely insights so often fade, I began to record them. Scraps of sticky notes with scribbled insights and longer thoughts recorded in a simple Word document over several years, accumulated into a book! (Never underestimate the power of tiny movements.)

Over time, I noticed the insights all pointed me back to one source, God. Being completely honest, I had fallen asleep on the job as a Christian. Low expectations, repetition, and worldly worry had created a weary heart and mind. The good news is that we don't have to stay there. Tiny glimmers had begun to penetrate my sleepy system. I savored and collected the tiny insights, worried I'd forget, and I became transformed one tiny revelation at a time.

What you have in your hands are random musings that plucked my heart in such a way as to encourage me to think differently about nearly everything. Changing the way I think, I slowly began to wake up and level up. I'm learning, however, that not everyone wants to level up. Many are very content to stay fixed in the exact mindset and location they have been in all their life. If that's the case, you'll read this book and be entertained by Charlie. I'm also learning that some, (including myself till very recently), were completely oblivious to the deep and blinding haze of complacency they had settled into. My hope is that you will take these revelations and make them your own. Pause, ask, listen, seek, awaken, own, and apply them to your life, your family, your thoughts, and, ultimately, you'll wake up to a new and better relationship with the maker of your very soul.

Read a chapter a day or once a week, or if you're like me, you'll want all the downloads all at once and you'll devour it in one sitting. But be sure you take the time to pause and ponder. Gathering knowledge and not allowing it to change you is simply a waste of time. Begin conversations with your loved ones and, even better, stir up a conversation with God, if it's been a while. I've added sections at the end of each chapter to help you think and to inspire you to dig deeper. Ask the hard questions and really contemplate the answer. Let truth seep in one precious and powerful word at a time. Let it transform you, too! What I learned is not just for a boutique owner momma in Southern Pennsylvania, but it's available to you, too! Honestly, I gathered the insights so I wouldn't forget the lesson. This book is my own wordy way of building tiny monuments to celebrate and remember. But if you, too, can pick up a few new insights and revelations, it's a glorious win!

If you're anything like me, you'll want more information. I started to voraciously devour books, sermons, the Bible, and YouTube videos until I became overly busy yet again, even in the good stuff. It seemed everyone had an opinion-- some good, some questionable. I was overwhelmed about where to go, which book to read first, and which opinion was correct. The tendency is to throw up my hands and keep doing things the old, familiar way. My best advice is to go to the Source. Crack open that Bible and ask Holy Spirit to help you understand. Read it with Him, speak it out loud, write down scriptures that poke your heart or jump off the page, and memorize them.

Time with Him isn't just for Sundays. He wants to do life with us all the time, every minute. Life with us is called Communion and it's not just crackers and juice at church. It's so much more! The ultimate revelation of gathering these tiny insights is that He wants to be with us, He's always talking, and if we take the time to listen, we'll truly hear Him. Charlie simply helped me slow down enough to listen.

And, by the way, if you don't know Jesus, you should, He's awesome. The truth He has for you won't transform you into a boring fun-killer. In fact, just the opposite. He'll remove that heavy burden of old garbage, low expectations, sleepiness, and rote repetition, and teach you to walk in the best possible direction. Try Him out, you won't be disappointed.

Let's get to it!
Xo

Lisa

1

MEET CHARLIE AND ME

I never wanted a dog.

Growing up on a farm, my experience of dogs included fierce, always caged German Shepherds with warnings from my dad to keep far away. My husband, Tim, however, grew up with a house dog, and since the kids were young and wanted the whole dog experience, off we went in search of our own!

At the Society for the Prevention of Cruelty to Animals (SPCA), we searched for a small-sized Pug and came home with a medium-sized Puggle named Charlie. (A Puggle is a mix between a Pug and a Beagle… he's a good mix of both.) While I filled out endless paperwork to even be considered as the adopting family, Tim browsed countless cages of large dogs and only a handful of smaller dogs.

The first dog we considered was a Jack Russell. We brought him into a test room with a couch and loads of toys to see if he would be a good fit for us. The dog, appropriately named Jack, was super energetic and paid us zero attention.

Tim mentioned there was an empty cage with a nametag noting a Puggle named Charlie lived inside. Charlie was out for a walk with volunteers. By the time we finished our energized visit with Jack, Charlie had returned. Bringing Charlie into the test room, he wanted nothing to do with toys and everything to do with us. He was thankful to be considered, loved being snuggled, and liked treats. He wasn't the cutest dog, but he was devoted. He had a pronounced underbite which made him appear deceptively fierce. Our collective senses flared; this was the one. So, we finished the paperwork (much like buying a car) and attached our leash.

Driving home, hearts full to overflowing with this new member of our family, I sat in the back seat while Charlie shook like a leaf. Every part of him, to his very core, vibrated. Never having an inside dog, I wondered, was he cold, was he afraid? Assuming both, I threw my arms around him, buffering him as the car rounded the corners, and whispering affirmations that every little thing would be alright.

Charlie was alert. Where was he going this time? The last car ride brought him to a cage. He was panting and I could feel his tiny heart fluttering. More affirmations, it's all okay, we're almost there. He sat at constant attention the entire ride home nestled directly beside me. He steadily peered outside, as if trying to remember the way home or attempting to find something familiar. More affirmations, more soothing sounds.

Nearly a fifteen-minute ride home, we arrived and introduced Charlie to our daughter, Maya, and our son, Cole, who was instantly smitten. Cole was 7 years old at the time and was thrilled at his new dog brother. Maya, on the other hand, was mildly disappointed … she wanted a smaller dog and Charlie stood knee-high on a grown-up. She was 9 and it took her a few days to warm up.

And so it remains. Charlie and Cole are brothers ... they snuggle and exchange low-grade growls at each other and Cole talks to him daily. Once, I caught Cole asking Charlie about "his own brothers. Did he miss them? Or would he prefer not to talk about that?" Maya has taken some time to warm up to Charlie. She acknowledges him as family and thinks he's cute, but much like me, she interacts in sporadic bursts. Charlie, however, remains consistently patient and devoted. He engages with Tim like the house dog he wanted ... they roll and tug, and they wrestle and bark at each other.

With me, Charlie waits. He comes to me for his answered needs: food, potty, water. He satisfies all areas of our needs. Most noticeably, he's devoted. He wants to be near us, he roams beside us from room to room, from floor to floor. Telling him, "I'll be right back, no need to follow me to gather a book or the vacuum from upstairs," still he rises and follows. No boogie man is going to get me while he's on watch. He barks at every passerby in devoted protection, staring back at us afterward for acknowledgment.

Bringing Charlie home that day was the beginning of many happy memories, he is a perfect fit for our home and an integral part of our family. He roots, he connects, and he grounds our family. He provided a daily routine, also providing a break from the regular to pause, look around, and be thankful.

I'm not always the best family member to Charlie, but from day one he was devoted to us, paying us good attention, being patient with us, and showing us unconditional love. That day, he rescued us. He rescued me.

More to the point, I've always been a Jesus girl. Sunday school and summertime Vacation Bible School were regular in our house growing up. I wandered away from church in my youth but returned to Christ once Maya and Cole were born, wanting our children to know God. He will use every single possible thing to be found; for me, it was the kids and Charlie.

Being the family member that spends the most time with Charlie, while the others head for work or school, I've been able to capture mini-lessons from our wise pup and how they so often point me back to God: the way He loves us, things He wants me to know, nudges to pay more attention to the good things and less attention to distractions.

Often these dog / God lessons were so obvious that I started making note of them, knowing I'd very likely forget them and have to be taught, yet again, that important lesson. These incremental lessons have carried me in the right direction, but I still have so much to learn.

These are but a few of the many lessons Charlie taught me about God.

2

CHARLIE AND GOD

Charlie is a good dog. He doesn't chew on my furniture or try to sleep on the couch. (At least, not that I'm aware of. Who knows what adventures he enjoys while we're away?) He doesn't mark the house with potty deposits except when we've been slack in paying attention to his nudges. He likes people for the most part (the innocent passers-by or bike riders are clearly dangerous threats to our household). For the most part, he is good. Compared to the potential wildness of other dogs, he's a really good resident.

He likes to snuggle, sleeps most of the day now, and doesn't leave demolished toys strewn everywhere, as he's not wildly interested in toys. The only downside I can recall is the massive amount of dog hair across the floor, and the snot strewed across the front windows, doors, and molding near the pantry door. All clean-up-able. A quick sweep of the floor and a motivated swipe of the windows and all evidence of his bad habits are forgotten. We're all glad to have Charlie. When we see other dogs, hyper, super barky, some that bite, some that are super anxious, we're thankful he's pretty chill. He's a good dog.

I can compare the characteristics of God to Charlie for a good long time, but when I attempt to compare Charlie with the person of God, things fall vastly short. Just as I said Charlie is a good dog, I could say God is good, too. I could say that, by comparison, our God is so much better. The thing is, God is good, but He's also One who should be feared and revered.

There's honor in fear. God wiped out entire communities in the Bible, He is wildly jealous against the worship of other idols (small "g" gods), Jesus tipped over tables in the sanctuary, then He formed and used a whip against the shady dealers in the court. He's gangster. Wait, He created the gangsters so He's an OG (original gangster). He's all-powerful. He's everywhere and in all things. He holds all things together. Literally, without His presence, everything, including you and me, would fall apart into cellular mush.

God deserves honor and praise and our time and our love and so much more than I have. He deserves it all. In fact, angels right now are encamped around Him singing Hallelujah and have been since the dawn of time, not because He craves it or demands it, but because He's worth it. There's no one on this Earth I can compare to God.

To drive home my point … I have great respect for Bono, the lead singer for my favorite band, U2. I respect his talent, his longevity, his perseverance, his charitable heart, and his ability to connect and inspire, but even Bono can't compare to God; He created Bono. Honoring Bono over God would be like honoring the gift wrap instead of the present. Our little half-activated brains can't comprehend that kind of presence, power, love, and honor. So, we trudge around this rock called Earth, finding rest, glimmers of Heaven in flower buds and sunsets (and other creations) and we too often bypass the bigger picture and the grander presence.

God is good because He is the original good. He created more good so it could point back to Him, the Source. God is love. He created more love so it could point back to Him, the grand and right and pure shape and presence of love. He is power. He is grace. He is patient. He is kind. And on and on. He's worthy of our praise and wonder and love. God desires us, He chases after us, He sings over us, and He has the ability to protect and shelter us. He offers peace that makes absolutely no sense (aka, surpasses understanding).

But it's us with our gift of free will who have to choose Him. We have to take that first step in grand surrender of belief and thus receive Him. Once He has residence, He'll begin to do some house cleaning. If you let him, you'll start to like the things

> *H*abits that kept you small and hidden will suddenly become unappealing.

that are in your best interest. Likewise, you'll start to dislike things that aren't in your best interest. Habits that kept you small and hidden will suddenly become unappealing.

You may lose friends. Let's just put that front and center. There are friendships that aren't in your best interest. God has a plan for you, a plan to prosper you and not for harm. Truth. And sometimes, the people you choose of your own free will aren't going to take you to that next level. Sometimes they want to keep you tethered to familiar ground. But safe and familiar aren't always best. I can tell you with great confidence because it happened to me. When some drift away, and they will, many more will arrive soon after. Ones who speak truth, ones who encourage, ones who will help you level up. God provides.

Lisa Weigard

In all this, God's presence and who He is scales enormous in comparison to Charlie, who is sweet and fluffy and all. But even Charlie was created by God and there's no comparing the two on the level of His person.

At this moment, Charlie is curled up, content, on my side of the bed where my pillow should rest. In these years together, Charlie has taught me so much about myself, about others, and about God.

Points to Ponder

What do I know about God?

_____

_____

_____

_____

Is everything I know truth?

_____

_____

_____

_____

Do I fear God?

_____

_____

_____

_____

Have I surrendered everything to Him? Why or what am I holding back?

_____

_____

_____

_____

3

PUTTING HIM FIRST

Some mornings, at the first sign of sleepy awareness when my eyes begin to flicker, I stay really, really still to see if I might squeeze in a few extra winks while Charlie sleeps. Most mornings, not so. Unsure if my breathing changes or if his internal timer is sounding, there he is, dark eyes unblinking, laying parallel to me, waiting to be fed and taken out for his morning potty visit.

It's clockwork. These things need to happen first, or huffs, tapping, and maybe even the passive-aggressive pawing at laundry will encourage me to move faster. He needs my first-morning attention. Everything afterward is extra, in his mind. So, I pull back my covers, and one foot then another touches the carpet, followed by my own morning bathroom visit. Then, it's off together to the pantry.

By then, he has nose-huffed approximately ten times, spraying dog snot in all directions, so I move quickly to reduce the sprays. By the time we reach the pantry, I'm hustling to turn the knob, swing it wide, right hand on the plastic dog food bin, lifting the lid, searching for the cup, filling it up, and pouring it into his bowl. Sometimes, halfway down, he nudges my hand, and food bits go everywhere. Other times his head is directly over the bowl, making it a push-back maneuver to get the food in the proper place. Then he feasts.

When he was younger, his food was gone in an instant. Now that he's older, he's taking his time. So, I wait, filling my own water glass, then more for him. I wipe down the counter from teenaged late-night snacking and wait for his highness to finish. Once every morsel is devoured, it's potty time. So off to the door we go. Jacket on, shoes slipped on, leash applied, and the door opened.

All the sniffs. The first spot is right by the door … who visited last evening? Always the same plant, as if it's a rendezvous spot - little spy notifications deposited for his nose only. Then the next bush, he's checking the perimeter like a good soldier. Then we're off to the mailbox and around the edge of the street, sniffing deep and long. Then and only then, does his daily deposit happen. It's a process and there's no rushing it. I've tried, believe me. These things need to happen first before his final donation can happen. So, I wait. I'm just along for the ride. He's the boss of this routine. I can try to rush any part of it and just end up frustrating myself.

And so it is with God. Any attempt to postpone my morning routine with Him to the afternoon or evening leave my days scattered, unanchored, and flurried. At first, it seemed like a task; yet another thing to accomplish in a long line of other important and unimportant things. But over time and practice, I began to notice the difference in my days and the lightening in my heart.

Whatever brings me there, the need for refilling, the quieting of the mind, God is there, always. It's me that needs to settle first to recognize where He is. Early on, in my morning time with Jesus, I tried creating a schedule: 7 a.m. prayer, 7:10 Bible, 7:30 meditation. It just became a checklist. I wasn't engaged. I wasn't communing. And I certainly was not abiding.

I'd never offer that kind of schedule to my very best friend, and definitely not to my husband, so why would I ever consider that would work for God? Yet, I followed that plan for months and wondered why, at first interaction, my bliss was zapped. He's too good and too big for a minute-by-minute schedule. So I released the schedule and let Him lead.

Just being in God's presence feels right. I will always hit my knees in gratitude for this new day filled with fresh blessings. I thank Him for His coverage and deliverance from evil and temptation. I ask for His daily bread (His daily delivery of fresh Jesus and/or His living and active Word somewhere in my day). I read His Word, slowly, stopping to ask questions, making notes, and pondering. I take a walk and pray over the country, the region, our churches, our police, health care, our government, our children, all children, and whatever pops in my mind.

> God is too good and too big for a minute-by-minute schedule. So I released the schedule and let Him lead.

Then I listen. I stop talking and listen to what sweet whispers He offers. What kind of friend would I be if I always did the talking and never listened? So, I stop my own words and listen for His. It's the sweetest time. Today, He told me I'm precious, paid for at a high price, valuable, special, worthy. That's the bread that will keep me filled all day. No one can take that away from me, ever.

God doesn't sleep, so I can just imagine Him, like Charlie, as I roll over and see Him staring at me with big, excited eyes.

> *I made this day for you! I can't wait to see how*
> *much you love it! Come, check it out!*
> *Let's talk, I missed you so much! I have so much to tell you!*

He deserves and desires to be first on my list.

Points to Ponder

What could I add to my morning routine (or take away) that invites God in?

_____

_____

_____

_____

What's the best way I feel connected to Him? (Do more of that!)

_____

_____

_____

_____

Who or what do I put first?

_____

_____

_____

_____

Do I ever feel like something is missing?

_____

_____

_____

_____

4

TRYING TO BE GOOD

It bears repeating. Charlie is a good dog. I mean a really good dog. In fact, as I type, he's adorably lounging upon his over-stuffed dog bed, super close to where I sit. A soft snore is sneaking from his wee pug squished nose and, every so often, his soft fuzzy legs let out a little twitch. He's cute right now, all asleep and easy.

It's when I'm finally feeling productive, when the juices start flowing in my writing, creating, or doing any single thing that requires my clearest, sharpest brain, that Charlie annoys me with false declarations of a potty break turned "gotta-sniff-the-curb" break. Instantly, my normally peaceful demeanor turns into a frustrated annoyed angry beast. And I know, I know, I know, the alternative is him spotting my carpet or creating a mess I'll have to tackle. So, I should be grateful for a dog that talks. But it takes such effort to get me to a place of settling down, to focus and obey, only to have it broken by a tapping or a huffing pup. In typical fashion, I aggressively scoop up the leash, apply the clip to his collar, and grump out the door. I walk him sternly. No sniffing, no walking the whole yard, just pee and poop and let's be done … all in a rush to return to my task.

And nine times out of ten, I appreciate the fresh air, the break from the task, but still.

I like my schedule; I like the flexibility of getting things done in my timing. I like dictating my day … and there lies the problem. I'm too in charge. More specifically, I like to be in charge. I don't like being told what to do. Charlie doesn't mind, it seems. He lines up in perfect routine, waiting for the clip to be attached to his collar, for me to slip into flip flops and throw on a jacket, unlock the door, his nose always pressed into the opening crack, so eager to move forward. Content. Appreciative. Anyone else would recognize the angst, shame, and fear and instantly distance himself, giving me wide berth until I'm calm again. Not Charlie. So, now I feel guilty. Somehow, once outside, I'm grateful for the fresh air, the sun on my face, and deep breaths of air.

I'm realizing I just don't like being told what to do. I don't like being pulled from the tasks I want to accomplish. Right now, I don't want to help one more creature. Ack. I said it. I give, give, give, and Charlie is always my breaking point. The most tender and sweet dog is the one place my frustration falls. It's like the toddler that's always good with the teachers and friends, but at home, he's a holy terror. It's the one safe place to let out all the daily tension, the mounting fear, a place to be real. And I know Charlie won't talk back or think I'm a hot mess, he keeps my secrets safe.

I don't like this version of Lisa … so I try harder to be softer. I pet him more (which he always avoids because it's a strange interaction from me – insert sad face). But ultimately all my trying is futile. Me trying to be kinder, me trying to be softer, me trying to be less frustrated only leaves me more frustrated. All the deep breaths, all the focusing on the good, any amount of self-generated calm flies out the window the minute I'm interrupted once again for food, potty treats, or the passing UPS man.

I've tried making better lists, meditating on pretty things, and taking long inhales. I can't do it on my own, as my efforts are shallow and quickly emptied. I've read way too many books, downloaded countless podcasts, watched endless YouTube sermons, and listened to inspirational speakers all in attempts to figure out the best possible way to navigate this life and be the best possible me.

Each great idea quickly fizzles. The next stirring message wrangles me to be more motivated. I'll do it better this time, I'll stick to it with beefier lists, I'll buy the best planner, and I'll dedicate time for all the necessary growth ingredients. Too soon the planner grows dusty, motivational sticky notes are buried beneath others, and I'm back at square one, frustrated and defeated. It's all self-driven, it's all based on me, me, me; getting me motivated and activated, all in my own understanding, my own efforts. I think I've got this life thing all figured out: say your prayers, read your Bible, smile a lot and be kind. The basics are just the beginning. So, I crank down even tighter and listen to more podcasts, read more books, and hang out with more Godly women. Still not the right track, even though they're all good things. I've still missed the target. There's way too much me in that scenario. I've chosen things instead of choosing Him.

Surrendering requires that I trust God. Trusting requires that I know God.

In fact, there's nearly nothing of lasting value I can do well on my own. If I'm completely honest, the majority of the good things I've accomplished are through the assistance and provision of God. His version of patience is so much better than my own self-contrived version. God is limitless and based on love, not gain or appearance. His version of love, in fact, is so much deeper, so much wider, so much higher, the bounds of which can never be tapped. My version of love runs out quickly and often looks for return, always looks

21

to love those more like me, and shelters safely within the confines of my itty-bitty understanding. On this journey with Him, the one life-altering method of change I've found is surrendering to Him. Waving the white flag, I relinquish control of trying to figure out every single thing and making every single person happy. Not my responsibility.

Ouch. I can only imagine the collective release and the collective clench that statement invoked.

Back to the basics…shelving everything else, the Bible study, the meetings, all the fluff, I've not been listening for His voice, the most important thing. Clearing the table of all the distractions, setting aside my constantly growing to-do list, I quiet my mind to hear God's still small voice. He's the best Boss. He's the best Father. He's the best Teacher. All other things are just a distraction. So I sit, and I wait expectantly until I hear the next task. Without distraction (most of the time), I obey, and then I'm still for the next task.

Only when I'm super close to Him do I learn what it's like to really love. Only then do I really reflect His character. My own character is rusty, His is perfect. I'd much rather carry His reflection than my own version. So, I snuggle in, push away the distractions, and listen closely. I dedicate early morning moments to reading His Word with the help of the best teacher ever, Holy Spirit. (How did I ever read it solo?) I ask for His opinion throughout the day on topics big and small.

My futile attempts transform into effective growth once I completely surrender to Him. There's nothing of lasting value I can do on my own efforts, so I push the self-help books and daily mantras aside, climb up onto the altar, and surrender myself to Him over and over again.

When I know and trust Him, I'm less likely to pick up burdens once I've laid them down. Trusting Him means letting Him tell me what to do. And in my getting closer to Him, I've discovered He's the best one to tell me what to do. I don't seem to mind it from Him … I don't always obey in the quickest timeline, but I'm learning to listen.

God's voice will never condemn, nor command anything not already in His Word or in alignment with His character (kick to the curb anything unlike Him). I'm learning, but I'm not perfect. Each day, I'm retraining my brain to do all the things differently, no longer in my own efforts, but directed and sustained by Him. Thankful for God's tapping and huffing, He's so patient with me to wait again and again and another thousand times while I continue to clumsily wear the boss hat. He knows exactly what I need. He waits for me to settle right beside Him, hooking up to the Source and taking a little walk together.

Help me Lord, to become more like You.
More patient, more loving, not only to Charlie but to all.

Points to Ponder

Where am I frantically busy? Do I feel overwhelmed? In what areas am I striving to be better, live better, do better?

_____

_____

_____

_____

What would it look like to surrender these things to God? How do I not pick them back up?

_____

_____

_____

_____

In what ways can I get closer to Him? Do I know what His voice sounds like?

_____

_____

_____

_____

How can I adopt His character over my own?

_____

_____

_____

_____

5

REST AND NOTICE GOD

Charlie doesn't chew the furniture or my shoes, although he does devour my underwear if left unchecked. He doesn't mark territorial spots around the house. He barks violently at each passerby ... big dogs, small dogs, runners, bikers, UPS drivers, the post office lady; all clearly without any weapons. Most often he sleeps. He's pretty easy to manage.

But by 5 p.m., I'm personally tapped out. His presence grates me. Blaming it on a thousand potty walks (honestly three), and incessant barking to be fed (only that final hour), the real culprit is me. Charlie is just the closest and easiest victim to deposit my frustration. Frustration at being ineffective, too much procrastination, lack of focus ... and by 5 p.m., the reality of the second shift settles in. Time to make dinner, head out for the next event, do the next thing, and my time for day work is done.

I learn and relearn this better way, forgetting it the next day to be gently reminded yet again.

Poor Charlie is the oblivious recipient of my self-frustration. He takes it well. He continues in a state of unconditional love, and a sweet expectation of any scrap of affection. I'm just mad at me and dump it all over Charlie. He's always there, always noticing, always loving. But I'm so self-focused that I typically miss it. Overlooking love, instead, I dismiss and discard it.

Being personally selfish by nature, Charlie reminds me there's a better way. Thinking I have it all figured out, my methods are to energize, pound it out, work, work, work, strive, strive, strive, and eventually, all the things will come into alignment. Just a little more work and striving and I'll have it all figured out. But the opposite is true. It's more rest, more noticing, more slowing down, more gratitude, a little Charlie petting, a few snacks, and maybe a nap and lots of love that place me in that happy spot. Instead of struggling and striving, Charlie reflects a better way, a way of rest and expectation. I fight it with every fiber, assuming my two-legged, upright superior position knows better than Charlie. I learn and relearn this better way, forgetting it the next day to be gently reminded yet again.

Charlie and God are faithful and patient with me. I can so easily put my nose to the grindstone and attempt to eliminate some portion of my overflowing to-do list. Yet I never feel fulfilled or accomplished, as tomorrow there will undoubtedly be more to do and likely someone or some dog on which to deposit all my frustration.

Taking a pointer from Charlie, the one most important thing begins with resting, noticing, and loving God. God is everywhere. He's in the flowers and the folding of laundry. He's in the wind and the whistling of the morning tea pot. Eliminating the busyness and fostering a grateful heart is a great first step to hearing from Him. He's always whispering the next task to be accomplished. Far too often, I distract myself with twenty other insignificant tasks creating confusion and frustration. If I'm completely honest, God's tasks bring exponential rest while all the distractions drain and fatigue.

On the rare days when I'm most obedient, waive the white flag, notice, and converse with Him all day long, I'm the most efficient, feel the most at rest, and leave more margin for noticing Him.

Tasks two through one thousand simply hinder, blind, and occupy the mind in a way that robs the ability to hear God's voice and see His good works. Those extra distractions frustrate and distract me, leaving an empty Lisa at end of the day. It's only when I do that one most important thing (and that thing is so unique to each one

> *Charlie has it all figured out. Every little thing will surely be all right. Obey, rest, savor.*

of us), that I'm in the right place to receive. To receive His peace, to receive His wisdom, to receive His presence. Everything else is extra and unnecessary.

When I'm obedient, I find rest. When I find rest, I find Him. It's a delicate and super-worthy dance I so often demolish with distraction and worry.

Rest doesn't always look like a nap. Rest is trusting that God has me in the palm of His hand, He sees me, and He'll never leave me. Rest invites a giant exhale and the ability to focus even more intently on only the most important things, letting all other distractions fade away, allowing that precious margin to seek Him out in nature, in His Word, and in His people.

When I'm not busy with a thousand tiny tasks, I see that monarch butterfly ... so intricate, delicately created in such perfection, and how it reflects God's order, balance, and beauty. When I'm not worried, new and creative understanding slips into the folds of my brain. When I'm not over-busy, I can hear His still small voice whisper life-giving truths.

Charlie has it all figured out. Every little thing will surely be all right. Obey, rest, savor. Once again, the life of a dog pointing me in the direction of God.

Points to Ponder

Am I frustrated with anything that robs my joy and keeps me striving?

_____

_____

_____

_____

What's my one most important task? (What is He telling you to do?)

_____

_____

_____

_____

What other things are simply distractions?

_____

_____

_____

_____

Do I trust Him enough to rest? What would rest look like for me?

_____

_____

_____

_____

6

LIVING LIFE TOGETHER

I may not be the family member that dishes out the grandest amounts of attention to Charlie every day, but that doesn't mean I don't love him. I care for him and want the best for him. I want him well and happy. I want all his needs satisfied. I want him to have the right amount of rest, food, and water.

Charlie is good. Perhaps the reason I do love him is because he is so good. Charlie's not difficult or troublesome. He's easy to love, especially when he's curled up right under Tim's chin at night or laying in sunbeams around the house throughout the day. It's simply so stinkin' adorable.

Tim might doubt my love for Charlie compared to how he expresses love towards him, but that doesn't change the fact that I do love him. I think Charlie appreciates the play and snuggle time from Tim and the taking care of business from me.

When we're all combined, the love we give Charlie ultimately checks all the boxes. He's part of this family. His bed is always beside the television, his own personal blankie lays right between my bed space and Tim's, and his leash and toys live in a basket by the front door. His little chain dangles and his tap-tappy toenails on the hardwood floors tell me exactly where he is at any given time. I can't imagine days without Charlie.

And so it is with God. I can't imagine life without Him. I can't fathom how others might rise without first saying thank you to Him, without touching base with Him throughout the day. I can't imagine savoring a sunset without considering the majesty of Him. But then, I realize we're all on different journeys at different points of the path, hopefully heading in the same direction.

God wants the best for us. He loves us on a level this world only once experienced, and even though it was nearly 2,000 years ago, that same love exists as strong as it did on day one. He teaches us that there is no greater love than for someone to lay down his life for his friends. And that's exactly what God did. He's good, and all the time, He is good. With all the endless variety of stress and strain that exists on Earth, trying to sojourn this life without Him seems hopeless to me. It seems exhausting and self-focused. On my own, in my own worldly flesh, I'd really only consider myself. Me, me, and more me. How short-sighted. How tiny and ineffective. I am good and satisfied and complete in Christ, but there are so many still struggling, still striving, still asleep. If I only focused on myself, how could I help those around me, and what would even be the point? Who or what would I be pointing them to if I didn't have Him? Life seems so empty and pointless without God and His never-ending, bottomless, fathomless, wide, and deep love.

I've gone through sad times. Times when I thought my heart would surely burst. But God surrounded me and sheltered me to allow me to do the task set before me. He's spoken sweet words of comfort in my most fragile moments. He snuggles up beside me, singing sweet songs when I'm most sad. I've gone through times of extreme worry, focused only on what's before me and forgetting His promises. He's guided me to safety, pointing me in the right direction time and time again.

> *We're simply not used to that level of love, but we're built for it; we're handcrafted to carry that kind of love.*

That's love. God loves me so much more than any of us love Charlie. It's grand and scandalous. Using worldly love, He shouldn't love us at all. We're self-focused, we return again and again to the stinky sin-laden places, even if just in our minds. We try again and again to do this life on our own. And being the loving gentleman He is, He lets us try. And yet, He loves us so.

My heart might nearly melt simply sampling a bite-size sliver of that sort of love. It's not something we see every day. It's not often passed down from our parents. Our version of love is conditional and fickle, depending on our mood. We're simply not used to that level of love, but we're built for it; we're handcrafted to carry that kind of love.

How sad that we, again and again, settle for so much less. I'll no longer settle for a second-best, garden-variety version of love. And just maybe, the more I allow Him to teach me about that love, I'll be more able and willing to pour out that same love onto others. Perhaps even a bigger dose onto Charlie.

Points to Ponder

How do I define love? Have I received God's love?

_____

_____

_____

_____

Where have I sold myself short on love?

_____

_____

_____

_____

Do I believe God loves me?

_____

_____

_____

_____

Do I love others the way God loves me? (Insider tip: If you think He doesn't love you, you'll likely not love others well. If you believe He loves you grandly, you'll love others in a big way.)

_____

_____

_____

_____

7

UNCONDITIONAL LOVE

Of all the dog-loving Weigards, I should rank lowest on the totem pole. Meaning, I don't change my voice into childlike tones when I'm talking to Charlie (like Tim). I don't lie on the floor to spoon with Charlie and speak soft loving words into his ears (like Cole). I also don't snap cute sunshine-filled pictures of Charlie and send them via Snapchat to my friends (like Maya).

Charlie and I have a very utilitarian relationship. We dance around each other giving food and wanting food. I give him a quick soft petting when no one is looking and succumb to the cuteness of his sunray lounging. I'm not heartless. But for the most part, I'm the least attention-giving person in the house. For the most part, I ignore him. I brush past him in a scurry to complete a task. I yell at him while he incessantly barks at the non-knife-carrying neighbors walking their dogs past our home. I give him the least possible amount of attention. And wouldn't you know, it seems I'm the one he loves and protects the most. My lukewarm love doesn't limit or shift his devotion.

Wherever I am, there Charlie is. As I'm migrating from level to level, room to room, cleaning the house, there he is. Pretending he's not afraid of the vacuum, he stays at my ankles. He stands in upright alert while I shower. He's always there, watching, waiting, protecting. When I'm sick, he insists on laying right beside me. When I'm sad, he licks my leg.

Of all of us, I would have guessed he'd love Tim the most. Once home from work, Charlie receives the bent down, both hands petting both ears, voice lifted an octave or two, "hey-so-nice-to-see-you-how-have-you-been-I-missed-you" greeting from Tim. My greeting to Charlie, by comparison, consists of a nod and a grateful exhale that he didn't poop on the floor, as I brush past him to drop my purse. One would think that greeting alone would make Charlie prefer Tim over all of us. But no. I'm his favorite, the one who gives him the least attention. He completely adores me in the most unconditional way. His love for me isn't dependent upon how much love I give him each day. He loves me regardless of how little attention I've paid. He loves me when I've ignored him all day long. He loves me in equal parts of attention and neglect.

And so it goes with God. Oh, how He loves us. He doesn't portion out or divide His love, He loves us with a never-ending, full tilt, overwhelming, doesn't make sense in this world, rarely ever seen, deep, vast, insurmountable variety of love.

And God doesn't pour out His love in bigger portions onto those who live large and super Christian. He didn't love Mother Teresa more and Hitler less. His is a scandalous love. He doesn't love us only when we love him. His is unconditional love. He seeks out those who are far from Him. He draws us in, keeps us close, and speaks soft words of truth in our ears. He leaves the many so He can rescue and return the one. Now that I'm in His tribe, I understand and celebrate the fact that He travels off to gather the other lost ones as I was once a lost one. There were entire sections of my life where I gave Him no attention.

I'm thankful God loves me so, even when I don't pay Him daily attention. When I'm distracted by the world-based enemy and go several days, sometimes months, without stopping to hear His voice or offer thanks, He loves me still. He loved me even in my darkest and most distant moments. He always has. I'm so glad He

> *G*od perches in protect mode, He rests in sunny spots, He curls up waiting for a snuggle, all the while knowing every single detail of my history, my thoughts, my heart, and He loves me still.

doesn't prefer the good Christians over this version. I could never live up to Mother Teresa's standards or speak electric and eloquent words like Billy Graham.

Here I am, typically offering the same utilitarian offerings that I do with Charlie…often a two-day touch: morning and dinner prayers and doing my own thing in between. Most days, I scurry in my own agenda, forgetting to touch base with God, overlooking the fact that I have access to the Secret Sauce of His love. And yet He loves me still. Very often, I completely forget to stop and listen for His voice or read His love letters. But still, He loves me. My tendency is self-focused, it's my neutral position. I have to purposely and intentionally shift my focus from me to Him. It doesn't come naturally. But still, he patiently waits for me to pass by, to pay attention, to pause. He perches in protect mode, He rests in sunny spots, He curls up waiting for a snuggle, all the while knowing every single detail of my history, my thoughts, my heart, and He loves me still.

I'm undone to the degree in which He loves, and I deserve none of it. But still, God loves me. And that fact, much like Charlie, makes me want to love Him more. It makes me want to search Him out, find out what He loves and do that stuff more. It makes me want to tell others how awesome God is, how loving He is, how they, too, aren't too far gone, and they aren't yesterday's garbage. They are yesterday's, today's, and tomorrow's treasure.

This knowledge should make me pay more attention to God. My heart and soul certainly want to give Him all the love, as the feeling and awareness of His love is better than any candy, more fulfilling than any other created thing. But still, that self-focused neutral returns, again and again, each morning and each moment. This is why He stresses the importance of renewing our minds. It's why He reminds us that fresh mercies emerge every morning.

I'm an internal wreck every single day, distracted, blinded, sleepy, with my worry balanced so often on the seen things and overlooking unseen power and promises. But still, God loves. It's who He is. He waits, He sings, He protects, He grieves. And when we pause and pay attention, He rejoices. Can you even imagine that kind of celebration?

We don't see that kind of love in the media, books, songs, or art. It's bigger and grander than anything we can imagine. It's extravagant, it's undeserved, it's scandalous. That kind of love should only be reserved for the top-notch and loving humans. Like Charlie and Tim. Charlie should love Tim most of all. Tim pays him the most attention and craves his presence.

If Godly love was based on attention, we'd all fall short. Thankfully, it's not. God loves even the worst of us. How could it be? Thankfully, I don't need to understand why, just that He does. And that knowledge makes me want to do better by and for Him. If I could realize that my love cup is already filled by Him each morning, I wouldn't seek it out in expectations from my family and friends. I'd dole it out liberally, knowing more was on the way. If I could realize I'm loved regardless of how much I get done or how well I complete tasks, I would be a bit easier on myself. If I could saturate myself in that kind of love, I would scatter it about on every single person all day long. But still, I fall short day to day.

Thankfully, He's patient, His love is unconditional, and today is a fresh day filled with fresh mercies. Knowing and remembering how much God loves me makes me want to pause more often and pet Charlie, enjoy His creation, and take in His daily, four-legged reminder of unconditional love.

Points to Ponder

Do I think His love is dependent on my works?

_____

_____

_____

_____

What lies about Him and His love have I believed? (Example: He doesn't see me. He couldn't love me. I'm too _____ to be loved.)

_____

_____

_____

_____

How would I move differently knowing I'm fully loved?

_____

_____

_____

_____

What is holding me back from receiving and acknowledging His unconditional and scandalous love?

_____

_____

_____

_____

8

RELATIONSHIP

As Charlie increases in age, he also increases in rest. Finding the coziest spot in the sun as it moves around the house, Charlie will shift, stretch, and adjust wherever the beams fall. He's not constantly nipping at my ankles or tearing up some precious thing. At this moment, he has gathered his personal fleece blankie in a proper nest on the top of my bed. Sometimes, the garage door will open, and he still rests upon his nest. We're able to sneak up on him; he's completely oblivious to our proximity. Maybe he doesn't hear us, maybe he trusts us finally. He knows by now that we'll come find him if he doesn't offer a door greeting.

That's relationship, I suppose; the see-saw balance of me coming to him and him coming to me. Me trusting that he'll find me if he needs anything, whether it's food or a touch. I know he's there. I can rise and find him for comfort if needed and he will seek me out for the things he needs. This relationship isn't a dictatorship where I proclaim the rules and schedules and requirements (although some days I admit I childishly wear that hat). Instead, it's a friendship. I care for his needs because I care for him. I want to take care of him because I love him. I don't want to overlook him for the entire day; not only because I know there'll be a big cleanup, but also because I care for his presence. I want him to feel loved, I want him to be the best dog he was built to become.

In this parallel of me and Charlie, which one is God and which one is the human? I'm not always sure if God represents the dog or the human here... maybe both. God rests and He interacts. He loves and receives our love. He comes to me and waits for me to come to Him. All the above and more. This, I know, is a relationship, not a dictatorship. God is not a bossy, finger-pointing, demeaning, condemning, heartless, fun-killer. He rests content, likely in the sun, waiting for us to find Him. He also jumps off the porch and over the front fence to pounce on us when we've been gone too long.

Being pursued and desired as part of a relationship makes me feel like I've been chosen for the best team ever, picked for the coolest friend group of all time. God is always there, any time of the day or night, ready to listen and console. He desires to hear all my juiciest stories, the sad ones, the big ones, the itty-bitty teeny ones. There's nothing He doesn't want to receive from me, good, bad, or ugly. The more I know God, the more I love Him. The more I seek Him in His Word, among His people, and in His creation, the more I find Him. I want to be loved by Him, and I want Him to know I love Him, too. Becoming the best possible version that He built me to be is a natural by-product of seeking and finding Him.

I've had barely-there friendships before ... the kind that weren't nourished but were left dormant and dusty. Those kinds of friendships lacked regular interaction and incorporated zero intimacy. When I leave out the most important parts of me in any friendship, what's left is shallow and fragile. That version of relationship is not the best possible version. One-sided relationships are not optimal either. Those are simply draining to maintain, where one is always wondering what the other is thinking; giving, and giving, and never receiving. Those sorts of friendships are exhausting.

Check God out. Give Him a follow. Sit and chat over tea one day soon. He'd love to hear from you!

What I've found and prefer are relationships that offer give and take in conversation, allow margin for quiet, and share the most vulnerable parts of one another's hearts. And that's exactly what I've nurtured with God. Years of Sunday and holiday touches with Him were just okay. They were good for a short season, but not good in the long term. A checklist interaction with Him was also a good start, but not the most optimal. I wouldn't interact with any of my best friends in a to-do type format.

When I cleared the decks, surrendering my preset notions of how to best talk to Him, no longer using scripted prayers and feasting on other's good interactions over finding my own, only then did I start seeing relationship roots begin to sprout. The roots spread quickly, and I began to discern His voice throughout the day. I began to desire His voice over other distractions. I began to understand the Bible more clearly. I learned to share the highlights and low points of my day with Him. I began to trust Him with everything. And that is the exact location He desires us to be. Check Him out. Give Him a follow. Sit and chat over tea one day soon. He'd love to hear from you!

Points to Ponder

What are my best relationships? Why are they my best relationships and how can I grow and improve in these relationships?

_____

_____

_____

_____

Do I need to find better, healthier relationships?

_____

_____

_____

_____

How can I grow in my relationship with God?

_____

_____

_____

_____

What kind of friend am I to God right now? How can I become a better friend to Him?

_____

_____

_____

_____

9

SO CLOSE

Tapping away at the keyboard, finally doing that one whispered task He wants me to accomplish today, I detect a steady shuffle-sniff, shuffle-sniff sound nearby. Charlie has pulled his substantially overstuffed bed into the sun, closer to me. He's only content by my side. The entire house is his to roam, and while he often disappears to gather random crumbs deposited by our teenage son and his friends, he always returns to my side.

In typical home-maker fashion, I'll shuffle from floor to floor, restocking towels, picking up laundry, grabbing something I've inevitably forgotten from my last trip upstairs, and Charlie is never too far behind. No point in trying to convince him to STAY, that I'll be right back, that I won't be too long. There he is, jingle-jangling right at my heels. I'm his girl. Even though

> *It's the way God prefers to work, woo, and wow the world. No longer residing in some far-away place, He's as close as a whisper. He hears His name, and He knows mine.*

I'm the one that shows the least amount of love, the minimal amount of petting, he loves me.

That kind of love is so rare.

But that kind of love is not rare with God. His favorite place is right beside me, or now as a believer, His most preferred spot is directly within the chambers of my heart. There's no place He'd rather be. He prefers to be carried around in the temple of this greying, slightly squishy, moderately smart, moderately efficient human. It's the way He prefers to work, woo, and wow the world. No longer residing in some far-away place, He's as close as a whisper. He hears His name, and He knows mine.

That nearness is a reflection of His love. His love doesn't depend on things done or said. Unaffected by how low I set the bar, He pours out abundant love regardless of return. That's Godly love, the kind of love He created originally because that's exactly who He is. He knows no other way than to love. There's no alternative, no G-rated, B-version variety. He loves because He is love. On days when I don't acknowledge Him at all; in moments when I completely ignore His suggestions; when I ignore His invitations to come closer and enjoy His presence, choosing chores instead, still He loves.

His is a variety of love so rarely seen in this world, but as close as a breath away. Amazing and scandalous love. By my standards, He shouldn't still woo me. I would have given up on me long ago, but still, He draws near, rescues me, surrounds me, and sings over me.

> *Lord, may my selfish and hardened heart be softened*
> *to accept and return that level of love.*

What a waste, otherwise. Yet we were never a waste. Paying the largest price to be this close, He places great value upon us.

This indwelling God joins us in our daily lives. He whispers while I fold the laundry. He comforts me when I experience loss. He alerts me when things aren't in order. The trick is to listen. To quiet the mind enough, to step away from distraction, and to be expectant for His voice. It's always there. Like Charlie's jingle-jangling dog tags and clippity-clapping toenails on the hardwood floor. But unlike Charlie, who rests more and more in his old age, our God never rests. He's always poised for a conversation. He's always eager to listen and speak. He's willing to provide insight, strategies, comfort, wisdom, direction, and more. His proximity brings peace. Days when I feel no peace are days when I've mentally or physically strayed from Him. So, I pause and search for His peace, waiting expectantly for it to land, then I move strategically and selectively around once again. Many of my years were spent without finding Him first; the alternative is so much better. No longer desiring to struggle and strive, I stop and seek instead.

So, as I look down at Charlie, finally content with his position in the sun (I did finally rise and help him position the bed closer...the effort was too much!), he's content, he's restful, he is love personified. Pondering the love that Charlie represents gives me a tiny flicker of what God must feel for me. I'm His girl, too, and have been His girl long before I was stitched together in Linda Kaye Elliott's womb. His is an everlasting love from way, way back. What Charlie offers is such a small-scale version, but it's enough to fill my heart with that warm mushy, soft, and delightful overflow of awareness. It's only a flash, a glimmer of realization, but it happened, and it was good.

I'll keep looking for more glimmers, more realizations of what God thinks of me, how He wants me to move in this world, and how much He loves me.

Points to Ponder

Do I believe God is nearby?

_____

_____

_____

_____

When have I felt His Presence?

_____

_____

_____

_____

How can I draw closer to Him in the busyness of each day?

_____

_____

_____

_____

Have I shared with Him all the "best-friend" topics?

_____

_____

_____

_____

10

ALWAYS NEARBY

Rising early, I feed Charlie, let him out for his bathroom loop, set out Tim's vitamins and juice, then sliver back into bed. A confused but content Charlie nestles snuggly into my belly. Listening to the rain, enjoying my warm pillow, and now in a content snuggle, Charlie and I enjoy a bit more sleepy time together.

Finally, it's time to rise and he performs his yoga-perfect downward dog and pounces off the bed to follow me on my circuit of morning duties. Tapping behind me while I go live on social media, following me upstairs for my slippers, he pulls his cozy bed beside me when I finally settle into my work spot. Not content to be six human steps away, he prefers to be within eyesight, even closer, within arm's reach. Charlie is dedicated and brilliantly positioned between chair and pantry, in case I'm feeling extra lovey and want to donate extra treats, or in case any of my work snacks find themselves on the floor. But more truthfully, he prefers to be right beside me. It's his favorite place. When all his humans are home, nearby is his most content location.

Once Tim arrives home and after dinner is complete, we typically lounge and chat about our day or fall upon the couch and zone out with some television. Wherever we land, Charlie insists on having his bed right beside us. He'll tap the wood floor or any obstacle nearby, then peer at us to send the message, eyes unblinking and neck craned to watch for us to respond. Too often to count, Tim rises and tugs the plush, four-sided bed right beside us and with a satisfied exhale, Charlie spins and drops into a cozy curl.

And so it goes with God. His favorite place is always nearby. In fact, He prefers an even cozier spot, directly upon and within, giving up Heaven so He could restore our rightful place. His preferred location is communion - togetherness restored. He wasn't content to be six steps away. He'll never choose to sleep on the basement couch. God took every effort to pull His comfy bedding right beside us in the hopeful chance we'd trip over Him and maybe realize how awesome He is.

But most days, I move in my own circuit, oblivious to God's presence, taking Him for granted. On my best days, I recognize He's there, offer Him love and praise, gradually becoming more like Him: restful, at peace, committed to love.

It's a grand mystery ... He came to set us free, to make things right again. It would have been enough to heal us, to split the veil allowing direct communication with Him, to teach us how to live and love. But the best gift was for us to become the temple...now we carry Him.

God desired to walk with us in the cool of the morning once again and He snuggled up within our hearts. More scandalous love and one grand mystery. I'm constantly amazed by His limitless creativity to offer previously unconsidered options. Who else would have found a way to

> *As close as a breath, as close as Charlie in a tight snuggle, God is always and ever so nearby.*

make us His walking temple? We carry Him into every family gathering. He comes with us to the store. He walks with me and Charlie. We bring the King!

There's nothing God doesn't want to experience with us and, oh, how I've fallen short of that awareness. He's seen my hangry short fuse, my impatience with Charlie, and worse. He is always nearby to talk it out, to receive my shortcomings into His ample hands. If I walked fully aware of His presence, the nearness of Him, I'd walk taller, prouder, constantly connected, and more aware of love. It's much like our pinky toe … it's always there, mostly silent, unaware until now. Now you are fully aware of your tiny pinky toe. It's all you can think about, right?

What if we shifted our attention to our Love-filled Inhabitant? What if we paused for peace before moving? What if we asked Him for insight before speaking? What if we praised Him for all the sparkly things? As close as a breath, as close as Charlie in a tight snuggle, He is always and ever so nearby.

Points to Ponder

Have I received Jesus into my heart and life?

_____

_____

_____

_____

How often am I aware of His presence?

_____

_____

_____

_____

Do I realize I carry the King?

_____

_____

_____

_____

How does His presence change everything?

_____

_____

_____

_____

11

DISTRACTION

Charlie pulls and pulls, eager at the leash, wanting to go faster than my casual stroll will allow. What is he straining towards? More smells, more lawns to mark, perhaps a pup friend? I maintain the pace, a nice, easy step by step, one in front of the other, patiently waiting for the determined sniff, two steps followed by more sniffs. I wait. He pulls a sharp curve to the left, another sniff. The path is straight, yet Charlie sways a thousand different ways. Sniffs here, marks there, a long stink-eye stare towards the woods, then a squirrel lunge.

He's not a good walking dog, and definitely not a good running dog. I'm often jealous of my friend Cara's dogs who run with her. I picture them trotting at a gentle Instagram-friendly pace, orderly following in one straight line while she writes books in her brain. Not Charlie. Sometimes he's on the left, sometimes he's on the right, and sometimes he circles around behind me causing a sneaker ballerina twirl followed by a frustrated leash shortening. It's hard to track, and it's even more difficult to assume where he'll be next. Distracted by scents, sounds, and senses, Charlie is a sugar-loaded toddler.

Distracted from his task by a million different things, big and small, far and wide, always looking, always taking in all the smells, all the textures, all the sounds. Charlie is me. Distracted by a thousand tiny things, veering off the path to investigate some curious pile. His brain must race through all the elements: That doesn't smell right! What's that sound? What's she doing over there? I don't like walking over that grate. Wait, gotta pee! That's me.

Circle back around Lisa, what was the original task? What's the one most important thing? Ah, there it is. Back to solid ground and on task. But then I'm thirsty, checking my phone on the way, and since I'm sipping, I might as well be snacking. An hour later, what was I doing originally?

> *O*n deeper reflection, my distractions are simply my own exit strategy into disobedience.

This way of working and thinking certainly isn't God's best for me. So, in typical fashion, it becomes a learning experience. As a believer, I have the mind of Christ, but I certainly don't fully utilize it. Instead, all that resource sits idle, unused, and dusty. On deeper reflection, my distractions are simply my own exit strategy into disobedience.

I know the one thing I should be doing, yet I don't do it. The apostle Paul struggled too. He lamented, "The thing I should do, I don't; and the thing I shouldn't do, I do" (Romans 7:19). I get you, Paul! I know what I should be doing, and I don't. I'm not really thirsty or hungry; I don't truly need a social media scroll brain break.

It's all distractions from doing the one most important thing. That one tiny whisper He delivers each day is the exact thing that I consistently avoid for a thousand untrue reasons. He whispers, "Write," and I find a mountain of fruitless tasks to accomplish instead. Avoiding the distractions sounds as simple as saying no. Truly it requires discipline. No, more than that! It requires surrender and accepting that He knows best so I will sit and obey. Ouch. There, I said it. The one word no stubborn human wants to hear … obey. When I'm obedient and do the one most important thing, it's as if everything else matters much less. This most worthy work will always be the most interrupted task. A book about God. Of course, the enemy would love a delay! Falling for his interruptions, allowing them to become distractions, I'm off task and all my momentum and all my

> Interruptions are just distractions I decide to accept. Interruptions are everywhere; obedience is required.

obedience sit untouched. On the rare days when I sort properly, getting the whispered work completed first and all else second, those are the days when everything falls into place and words just glide onto the page. But switch the script, and do my things first, then everything feels wonky; like parting my hair on the other side. Interruptions are just distractions I decide to accept. And both interruptions and distractions are tiny bites of disobedience. His whisper returns every single day only because I didn't obey yesterday. He knows best and still, I assume to know better. I'll do the thousand other things first, then I'll have time to obey. However, like digging a hole at the beach, something will always fill up the space. That one most important thing keeps glaring from my daily to-do list as the one most valuable, yet the one most likely to be dismissed.

What if our unique one most important thing is what's most needed to bring peace and connection to the world? What if this one thing will save even one soul? What if this one thing increases wisdom in a flurried mind like my own? And yet I dismiss it as small and allow interruptions the full access to enter in. Interruptions are everywhere, and obedience is required.

Interruptions will come, Charlie will need a potty break, he will need to be fed, and he will likely need a few soft and loving taps or belly rubs. But I must always return to that one most important thing. Someone, maybe even yourself, may benefit from hunkering down and doing the whisper work first.

As I'm typing and finally doing the thing He's whispered all day long for far too many months, distractions itch yet again. I should take a shower first, maybe a nice walk with Charlie, what are my Instagram peeps posting today? The distractions pick and nag right at the fringe, nonstop. But here I sit and ignore them while I keep my fingers poised for the next profound line or perhaps just some witty story. Either way, I'm obeying and squashing the distractions.

I'm not sure if these words are more for me or for some other lost soul. But either way, while the writing remains my whisper, today I obey.

Points to Ponder

What is the one most important thing God consistently whispers? (Have you asked Him?)

_____

_____

_____

_____

What are my distractions that pick and nag right at the fringe, nonstop?

_____

_____

_____

_____

Why am I not doing that one most important thing? Is it because of fear, intimidation, lack of interest, or disobedience?

_____

_____

_____

_____

What would it take to finally do that one most important thing?

_____

_____

_____

_____

12

GENTLE NUDGING

Charlie has a unique system of getting his way. Not quite finished with our meal, trying to have a decent conversation, there's Charlie, peering at us with his unblinking steely gaze, his eyes increasing in size with his growing impatience, as if his endless dark eyes could compel us to rise immediately, walk to the pantry, reach for the treat box, and deliver one bone-shaped biscuit directly into his eager mouth. We all grow agitated when he huffs impatiently or swats at the Roomba trying to get our attention. You're not the boss of me, I think. Then immediately, I walk to get the treat. Well, not me. Usually, it's Tim who succumbs to the treat stare. Charlie has trained us, and he's insistent…he'll not stop until he's satisfied.

A similar routine begins at 3 p.m. or some days Charlie's "feed-me" routine begins at 1 p.m. We feed Charlie at 4:30 p.m. before our dinner begins so he's satisfied while we eat. This is not the case anymore since the treat stare-down began, but still. It's a several-hour routine of rise and stare, swat at the plant, then stare back at me for reaction. Oh, and please do not pass the pantry, the sacred location of his food, because he will think that surely you're there for his bidding. No? "I'll take care of that with my fixed gaze. No? Let me snort? No? I'll win this game," Charlie says. Usually, I win the game and feed him at 4:30 p.m. but not before I've become overly agitated and frustrated with the insistent and impatient hours prior. He wants his way and won't stop until it's done.

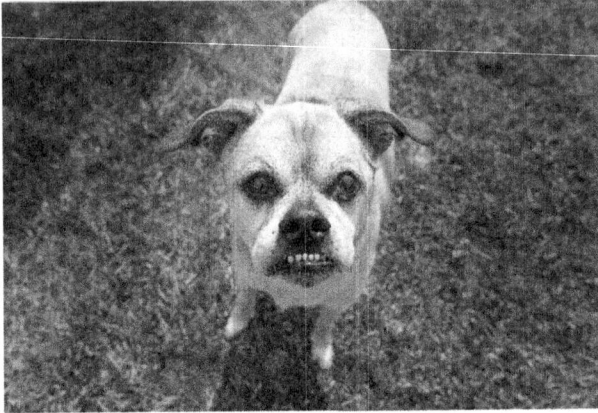

And so it is with God. If God stood before me, in all His flesh and bone glory, sometimes I think He, too, would give me a similar steely eye gaze for procrastinating this writing for so long. He whispers, "Write" every day and I place a thousand tasks before Him. Even seemingly good and true tasks. Assisting with Bible study, running a Propel class, cleaning the house, or watching a thousand YouTube sermons. All good, but all distractions from that one task He asks me to do each day. He's not nearly as obnoxious as Charlie, but He does send steady and consistent reminders. Little nudges through friends, connections I never could have gained on my own, planted in my presence to guide me towards that one whispered task.

Okay, okay, I give. Finally satisfied, in the place that feels most right, I plant myself in front of the laptop, position my hands upon the keys and wait for the words to flow. And they always do. I don't know why I resist so ferociously. He tells me where to go, which direction to point my boat, and tells me He'll meet me on the other side. There are no incremental steps required, write about this, say that, just write. And I know if He's given me a task, He's fully equipped me to do it, so my only effort is to show up and be obedient.

There's no need to check the inventory, there's no space for comparison or doubt, although both creep in and block the good flow all the same. Squash it and move on, back on track. His loving yet steely gaze will continue until the task is done. So, I sit and write, again and again, never knowing what will bubble up, but here I am. I know the good and necessary words will rise. It's my part to believe they will come. Anything extra is a delay, procrastination, and disobedience, it's a giant pressing of the pause button.

He knows best for me, and I deny it over and over again. He has good plans for me, plans to prosper and not for harm, but still, I think I know best. He has heard conversations I haven't heard, and He makes connections I cannot. If He tells me to write, there's a reason for it. It's not for me to argue, deny, contemplate, or disobey. In fact, there are side effects to disobedience. Other people will be given my task to accomplish, blessings follow those who obey, curses follow those who do not, and then there's rest. Sweet rest is available for us to enter if we aren't disobedient. It's in the Bible, take it up with Him (Hebrews 4:11). I don't want anyone else to finish the task He's given me, and I certainly don't want to open myself or my family to curses, so I sit, and I ponder, and I obey my one whispered task.

It's my whisper and nothing else will satisfy. Only when I rise and reach for the treat will the nudging finally stop.

Points to Ponder

What nudging have I received from God?

_____

_____

_____

_____

Am I denying His best for me? Why?

_____

_____

_____

_____

Have I been obedient to respond to His nudging?

_____

_____

_____

_____

What distractions have I allowed to interfere with my obedience?

_____

_____

_____

_____

13

STOP AND SAVOR

Charlie and I have a new routine evolving. I take a longer "prayer walk" alone where I talk half the time and I listen the other half. Then I return home, open the garage door, and call for Charlie so we can enjoy his portion of the walk. What started as far-away Charlie is becoming a waiting and listening Charlie. He now sits at the steps or at the garage door waiting for my return. He has learned to anticipate my arrival and his reward. (Who says you can't teach an old dog new tricks?!) Clipping on the leash, out the door we go.

Nearly every time, our path follows across the street and onto a grassy area near the mailbox that must be the landing spot for all kinds of messages for dog noses. It's approximately twelve steps and a full stop for an in-depth sniff. Taking it as an opportunity to breathe (as my last portion is uphill), I gaze around, enjoying the stillness. But after a few minutes, I'm ready to move again. Pulling his leash to lead him out of the deepest and clearly the yummiest scent, we walk one more step for yet another full stop. One step, stop; two steps, stop; it's the world's laziest country line dance.

I crave a steady walk, with legs extended into a full and lengthy gait. But no. Charlie is intent on gathering all the messages, missing not a single sniff. One-half step, pull back, stop. It's frustrating. I'm always so jealous of the dog moms with a pup that trots along nicely, in a straight line, not bothered by the many messages all around them. These mannerly pups seem neither intrigued nor distracted. Charlie savors every scent, every texture, every sound. Not true with his two-legged mom.

I am that gal who wants every single scripture promise delivered, who desires every single ounce of knowledge available, and who skips to the end of the self-help book to capture the bullet items hoping to jump right into fullness and goodness. Just tell me what to do and I'll implement and adjust. I don't need to know why, yeah, I know it's good for me to be healthy, happy, and wise, just let me skip to the doing. The doing gets me there faster, right? Charlie and relationships in general, including the one with God, turn out to be more like checked boxes than filled ones with this busy-based perspective. But I'm learning along this journey that God will take me one step forward and pause to savor the lesson, building our relationship by building trust, allowing lessons to saturate into the deepest folds of my brain, renewing old thoughts and ways. We've often knowingly or unknowingly allowed lies to creep in and lay crusty roots.

The Word is able to dig out the enemy's arrows; those deep and invasive lies that twist and manipulate the truth. The Word is able to illuminate dark places long hidden and carried as a secret burden. This weapon is too precious to dismiss and to only use lightly on Sundays and holidays. God is too precious to rush past. He is too dynamic to assume we have all knowledge from a few Sunday school classes. His love is too big to assume He doesn't see us. So again and again I will pause, savor His Word, break it down, add my name to each scripture, apply it to my family, and cast it out over future grandchildren and their children. I don't want to miss a single morsel.

It's far too easy to succumb to enemy distractions and overlook a peek into Heaven. Perhaps it's a good Word delivered by a friend, a single butterfly breaking up the view, a chance to recall some long-forgotten truth, to heal in a way that only He can provide. The alternative is to rush past, scurried, missing the juicy goodness, remaining only half-filled, looking holy yet shining no light, growing no good fruit.

Worldly Lisa wants to have it all, but Heavenly-minded Lisa is learning to let the lesson seep in deeply before moving onward. Picking up new messages among His people and in His Word, I'm learning to pause and ponder. I ask the questions. What does this mean for me? What do you want me to know? I've begun to pray before reading scripture that Holy Spirit will awaken the words and help me understand, remember, and apply. His Word is not only a love letter transferred through the ages, but it's also a worthy weapon to fight the enemy. The side effect to this process? Over time, Worldly Lisa is dying off and Heavenly-minded Lisa is beginning to thrive. I'm less likely to be frustrated at Charlie's pauses, his long sniffs, and his lazy line dance.

Charlie is reminding me to stop and savor. I don't want to miss a single lesson.

Points to Ponder

When was the last time I sat and read the Bible? Have I really dug into the Word?

_____

_____

_____

_____

_____

Where am I most distracted? Have I noticed I'm more distracted when I sit with God or when I read His Word?

_____

_____

_____

_____

_____

Do I realize I can ask Him in any interaction, "What do you want me to know?" (Ask Him now. Then ask Him throughout your day.)

_____

_____

_____

_____

_____

Why do I avoid quiet time and meeting with God? What am I afraid of learning about myself or finding out? How can I incorporate stillness into my routine?

_____

_____

_____

_____

_____

14

PONDERING

Charlie is good. He is patient and kind, he reflects long-suffering, and he is abundant in love. He isn't arrogant or rude, he doesn't hold my wrongs against me, in fact, he doesn't even remember them. Charlie is one of many perfect reflections of God. In fact, those reflections reside in all created things. Unveil the eyes and take a longer look … there God is again and again just waiting to be found.

How many times must I pass by Charlie and God without even a tiny acknowledgment? Even now, Charlie rests on my freshly laundered bed, kicked out sideways, softly snoring, likely drooling, completely safe and content; his surrender draws me in and compels me to pet him … to linger, to look and ponder. This four-legged creation has lived within our walls for over 10 years and still, too often, I overlook the wonder of Creation. Charlie's soft padded feet, sensitive to touch, perhaps ticklish? Those long black whiskers help him navigate tight spaces, with super-sensitive antennas. The variation of color from front to back includes tiny tornado swirls of hair growth. The neatly stacked teeth create a fearsome underbite, concealing his sweet demeanor. The wagging tail reveals inner joy when Tim enters the room or when I randomly draw near. His velvety soft ears are so satisfying to rub between my thumb and forefinger. So many wonders, so quickly overlooked with a passing glance or my typical annoyance.

When I set aside my own selfish thoughts, Charlie fascinates me. What other animal do we allow to roam our home? What other animal do we trust near our children? What other animal can be taught our routines? What other animal is so unconditionally excited to see us each day? Charlie is fascinating to ponder.

Pondering. It's a sweet luxury overlooked in most moments. Setting aside all distractions and looking deep within a flower is amazing. They return each year, adding color and fragrance to our world. Notice the passing butterfly … those beautiful wings splashed with symmetrical color, lightly drifting from place to place. Observe a starry sky … so vast and distant yet dotting our night sky with such beauty. All of it was created, held together, and intricately designed to point us back to Him.

One of the things I love most about Mary, the mother of Jesus, is that she often pondered things in her heart. She took notice of events or statements and considered them quietly. She chewed on truths until they became new and good thoughts. She treasured sweet moments and tasted them often. I have to wonder if a lifetime of pondering helped to ease some of the intense grief she experienced at the cross.

Originally, the word *ponder* was written as *sumballo*, which means to throw together, to bring together, to converse, to meet, to encounter in a hostile sense, to fight with one or to bring together one's property, to contribute, aid or help. Pondering brings previously unconsidered things into view. It takes one thing and marries it to another. *Sumballo* implies a more aggressive joining than just thinking about something. *Sumballo* is a wrecking ball against stale, dead, mundane thinking. Pondering as *sumballo* forcefully mashes two colors of play-doh, squashing, folding, and stretching until new colors are created. Multiple thoughts collide together creating something new. Lofty concepts begin to make sense. Two seemingly unrelated experiences suddenly smash into fresh revelation. New thoughts connect and cover old thoughts. Previously considered ideals marry together with new concepts. A crusty, dusty brain becomes invigorated and alive.

Awake, oh Sleeper! God can be found in all things, so seek Him out in nature, in His Word, in His people. Slow down to pay attention, listen, and recall. Don't just let the Sunday pastor read the Word to you. Crack open the Book during the week and seek out what each word means in its original language. Take notes in the margin. Look up the references. Ask what Holy Spirit wants you to know about this or that. He was sent to help and teach us, after all!

> *We* are surrounded by God's glory when we simply stop and ponder.

I've noticed time and again that the fiercest battleground is directly between my ears. The enemy loves to keep me distracted, dumbed down. And the very moment I notice something good, the inner chatter begins. (Why else can I become mindlessly engaged for multiple hours in a scandalous television series but find it difficult to settle down, focus, and read the Bible? Ponder that.)

Pondering is hard-fought. The enemy loves to keep us focused on other shiny yet meaningless things. Fight to ponder. We are surrounded by His glory when we simply stop and ponder.

Points to Ponder

What things have I pondered today?

_____

_____

_____

_____

What items in nature reflect God and His character to me?

_____

_____

_____

_____

What crusty thoughts need to be invigorated? (Take extra time with scripture to _sumballo_.)

_____

_____

_____

_____

Have I noticed God drawing me to ponder?

_____

_____

_____

_____

15

PLAY

He may carry much gray, but Charlie still has the ability to play! Most moments, you'll find him resting. But when Tim wants to wrestle or carry him like a baby or play tug of war with a toy, Charlie is willing and able! (Notice I said Tim and not me … I'm not the player for Charlie … I'm the feeder-walker-occasional-belly-rubber).

From the dishwashing position, I can hear playful growling, jumping, and pounding of paws on carpet in the front room. Those sounds usually mean Tim is on all fours playfully pouncing, offering soft jabs to the left and right, boxing with Charlie. So, Charlie in return gets in play position, backside up, shoulders down, eyes wide, mouth open, two pounces to the left, one pounce to the right. Let's do this!

Sometimes, Tim will grab a soft toy or rope and Charlie knows exactly what to do … he grabs one end while Tim has the other and he pulls with great ferocity, as if there was a baby in the well that needed saving. At the end of the play session, Charlie is either spoon nestle hugged or picked up and carried like a baby ... his favorite part. It's like he endures the play knowing the sweet snuggle awaits.

> *E*verything God created reflects some aspect of Him, so I can only imagine how playful He is as well!

When I attempt to play, Charlie is unsure of my intentions. He wriggles and pulls away from my reach. He avoids me because I'm not the player in the family. I figure so many others take care of that task, I don't need to check that box. I'm the business part of the relationship: vet visits, administering meds, picking up poo, buying more food and treats, doing all the things. So, why should I be surprised when he doesn't recognize my playful attempts? There is a definite balance between work and play and my tendency leans toward work. The playing and relating often seem secondary, seemingly a waste of time.

Everything God created reflects some aspect of Him, so I can only imagine how playful He is as well. After all, He created sloths and sunflowers, dolphins, and tickle spots.

Yes, God is all-powerful and grand, lives in unapproachable light, and He also causes great joy. And I've never experienced more joy than in endless belly rippling, pee a little, reckless abandon, laughing. I mean, to dwell only on the majestic things, like sunsets and mountains, oceans, and humans (I mean, wow, the intricacies there alone ...) would be considering only one part of His creation and thus, only one part of His character.

Scripture says that all creation reflects God's majesty. That means everything He created points back to Him, revealing some part of His nature. He is good, He is strong, He is able, He is detailed, He is perfect, He is almighty, He is powerful, He is tender, He is caring, He is patient,

He is all-knowing, He is larger than life, He is the great healer, provider, all of it … every single thing all at once.

The detailed flower reflects His perfection and provision, the wind reflects His power, trees reflect His firm foundation, each item revealing some aspect of Him. So, when Charlie is willing to play, while he still can in his creeping years, it makes me consider that yes, God even has a sense of humor. He loves to see us happy and playful. He instructs us to be like children, and kids love to play! It's good for the soul to laugh, release and rest from worry.

Even Jesus attended weddings … places of grand celebration, dancing, singing, telling stories, and laughing with friends while making new friends. He is not the wall-clinging, judgy, fun-killer the world suggests. Being a Jesus-girl, being a Christian, should reflect joy, not suppression. Our faces should light up dark places. Living life set apart as holy doesn't have to look somber and depressed. It requires taking away what the world sees as fun and replacing it with the things God originally created as joyful. Things that satisfy, things that bring rest, things that compliment and encourage, things that fill cups and do not empty them.

There's time for everything. The dishes do need to be finished, but not all of life needs to be so serious. And even in the daily tasks, our joyful hearts can accomplish them with excellence and not complaining. I do need to incorporate more play, more painting, more crafting, more walking and noticing His creations, and more belly laughs. Like so many others, I get anchored in the adulthood mindset and forget my childlike playfulness. Surely all the to-dos need to be completed, but Charlie is teaching me that perhaps even more important is the play/rest connection.

Without play, life is just business. Clearly, it's important to God for us to be playful, to release and be silly with each other, to laugh and surrender. It's good to tumble and wrestle, and it's even good to close it out with a good snuggle and maybe even a belly rub.

Points to Ponder

Have I forgotten how to play?

_____
_____
_____
_____

When is the last time I laughed?

_____
_____
_____
_____

What makes me laugh? (Do more of that!)

_____
_____
_____
_____

What reflects God's sense of humor?

_____
_____
_____
_____

16

KEEPING IT SIMPLE

On a daily basis, Charlie is crowned with the title of Diva. He prefers only the softest spots, pulls his bedding into the sun, loves to curl up on laundry fresh from the dryer, and expects treats for every good thing. He doesn't ask for much, yet he knows what he likes … everything else is extra. He doesn't complicate his life with a thousand must or should dos. He doesn't add commitments to his life that don't fuel or recharge. He doesn't wander looking for the next wonderful thing. He waits patiently for its arrival. Charlie keeps it simple. Tim and Cole have said more than once, "Oh to have Charlie's life!"

While I'm super glad to be a two-legged walker with a word-speaking mouth and a mind that grows wiser each day, there is a small part of me that's drawn to Charlie's simple life. Snuggle all night, rise for eats and potty, back to bed. Perhaps a walk later, sniffing every single thing, followed by some fresh water and another nap. Potty break number two, wandering around for snacks, trusting dinner will be delivered around 4:30 p.m. Yet another potty break followed by another. Maybe another nap. Then up to the human's bed. Only the basics remain. Nothing added, nothing taken away. The simple life.

At one season, my life was far from simple. I filled my plate with too many things. I'm a hard worker with a servant's heart. If there was a need, I filled it. I'm adequate and a quick learner. The plate fillings were all good things; volunteering at church, Bible study, organizing a clothing outreach. No single bad activity, but things not necessarily for me. I wrongly filled a space otherwise occupied by the right person. I jumped in without praying for guidance. I filled my time with activities as if earning a Heavenly VIP invitation.

That's not how it works. It's all completed. He loves me. Because I believe in Him, my sins are as far as the east is from the west. There's nothing He holds against me, and I can't earn an ounce more love because I'm currently at maximum capacity. I was at maximum the moment I believed, in fact, I was on love-overload

> *My* most productive times have been in obedience, doing that singular thing God whispers, followed by being still with Him.

even before I was knit together, and I will remain at that level even after my last breath. Every breath in between doesn't need to be filled with action. In fact, my most productive times have been in obedience, doing that singular thing He whispers, followed by being still with Him. Everything else falls right into place accordingly.

In the season of full plates, everything felt itchy and unsettled, I could tell something needed to change and, within nearly no time, I had completely cleared the decks. Having no commitments felt really liberating and opened me up to do the next most important thing, which was spending precious time with my mom as she left this world. I had no idea that was on the horizon, but He did. A clearing of decks was necessary to allow focused time with her. Afterward, I was deliberate with my time, allowing only the best yeses onto my plate, praying over every single potential addition, and confidently saying no to anything less than best. Keeping it simple has allowed me the margin to be still with Him, to notice Him more, to walk with Him in the mornings, to do the most important thing each day, and taking lessons from Charlie each day by keeping it simple.

I'm nowhere near perfect. I want it all and I want it now, but my most effective and restful position has been found when I'm like Charlie and work from a place of rest. My most profound days have been when I've kept things the simplest. I try not to add any unnecessary activity and I pause before jumping into any new commitment. Even doing good things can be an unnecessary distraction.

It's best to live like Charlie, doing only the most important things, resting often, hanging around good people, being grateful, and seeking Him. Keeping it simple.

Points to Ponder

Where am I too busy? Why am I so busy?

_____

_____

_____

_____

What can be eliminated or reduced from my schedule?

_____

_____

_____

_____

What is He telling me to do each day?

_____

_____

_____

_____

Am I trying to earn points or impress others with my busyness?

_____

_____

_____

_____

17

POO AND GOODNESS

Charlie pooped on the floor again. Seems the frigid winter snow is just too extreme for his precious rump. Immediately I'm enraged. Brand new house, freshly steamed carpets with four warm piles of dog poo. One more thing to do before I can finally sit down and listen to what God wants me to teach about today's Bible study lesson on God's goodness. Describing good right now feels like describing yellow to a blind person.

My unexpected task now flushed and hands washed, I finally sit and clear my mind. "Lord, what do you want to tell me about your goodness?" "*Why were you so mad at Charlie?*" He inquires. Pausing and pondering, I answered, "I have something nice, and Charlie makes more work, he makes it harder than it has to be, and he takes what's good and makes it messy". "*Hmmm...I see*". Suddenly aware of His methods, His way of asking questions to give lessons, my ears perk. "*Why else?*" I answer, "He had the chance to deposit his morning's waste outside, in the proper place, but instead decided to hold onto it and drop it in places he shouldn't." "*Uh huh. Sound familiar?*" Once mad, now convicted, I'm realizing that even Charlie's carpet deposits have something to teach me about myself and His goodness.

God gives us this beautiful world filled with everything we could ever need, tops it off with extras, and still, we complain. We overlook His goodness and find the faults. Instead of appreciating all the sweet treats this day holds, we worry about future things or distracting lies. We make life and love so much harder than it has to be, heavier than it was designed. We take what's good and make it messy through the twisting of His Word, by warping love, by squandering life. We make a mess of things daily. We judge and worry, we divide and damage, we ignore and dismiss. He has good plans for me and for you and I can guarantee it doesn't involve scurrying and worrying. So long ago, He created this world and us and said it was good. He doesn't create junk regardless of what the enemy yells.

> My morning routine should be incomplete until I've placed every single lie into God's hands.

Every ounce of the enemy dialogue should be deposited straight into the Father's hands. Yet, I hold onto things I shouldn't until they build up and land in places they shouldn't. Old grudges, fear-based worries, lies about my identity, any single not-good thing should be released in the proper place. My morning routine should be incomplete until I've placed every single lie into His hands and then repeat the routine over and over again. The only place for messy thoughts is directly in the hands of the Father. Time and again I become the frazzled wife when Tim arrives home simply because of a burdensome worry lingering too long in my brain and heart. I become the fearful mom when some small dread has occupied brain space otherwise meant for His truth. I hold onto things I should deposit obediently into His super-connected, all-powerful, and mega-loving hands.

His character of goodness was on display for me front and center this morning. His goodness is contagious, and it quickly turned my angry heart to mush towards Charlie because he's a dog, and he likely gave me clues to his need, but in my scurried state, I overlooked it.

In typical Good Father character, God used Charlie's accident as a teaching opportunity. I gotcha. Be grateful, keep it simple, and turn everything over to God. I may have struggled to define good, but I can see that He is good through His patience and kindness and gentle teaching with me. I can see His goodness in His endless provision for me. I can feel His goodness in the peace I carry into stressful situations. He is good and I need more of that in my life.

Points to Ponder

What lies am I believing about myself, about others, and about God?

_____

_____

_____

_____

What extra junk should I turn over to Him?

_____

_____

_____

_____

Where am I worrying?

_____

_____

_____

_____

Do I believe God is good? Do I believe He sees me as good?

_____

_____

_____

_____

18

FORGIVENESS

Yesterday, Charlie earned another chapter in my book. After a long, luxurious weekend with friends, my unpacked bags became Charlie's feasting ground. As a special treat, I brought two packs of Justin's brand chocolate peanut butter cups. In my mind, they are a bougie snack reserved for special moments and special people. They are truly decadent and a big level up from the standard orange and black, trick-or-treat version. I had eaten only one over the weekend, leaving three pristine and perfectly created rounds of chocolate and peanut butter goodness.

Sitting to write, I deposited my tote at my feet and began to type. Hours later, we left for dinner and Charlie began his decadent feast. When we returned, paper evidence of previously mentioned yumminess was sprinkled all over the floor. Feeling extra ravenous or perhaps a bit spiteful of my absence, he also shredded and half-digested one pair of my underwear. It was a gluttonous night for Charlie.

To say I was mad is an understatement. Beginning the cleanup, still fuming at the loss, I also worried about his chocolate consumption, knowing it's an unhealthy snack for dogs. And it was seriously good chocolate, did I mention that? Dark and yummy. Even more upsetting for a dog's tummy. And the underwear! Now reaching a handful of underwear consumptions, it was time to restock. I'm pretty sure I was more upset over the loss of bougie chocolate. Charlie did get a firm yelling.

The next morning, Charlie and I began our little dance of morning routines like clockwork. There was no timidness, fear, resentment, or grudge held. He was back to true love. I, however, was feeling guilty for the hollering. It was my own fault for leaving the tote exposed at dog height. I should have taken out the decadent treats when I first returned home. Anyone with a dog or small child knows to keep important things out of reach. Maybe I was tired, or maybe I was excited to share weekend stories, and the treats skipped my mind. I should have closed the closet door during dinner, too. It was my fault that Charlie had access to the smorgasbord. Yet he held nothing against me. My own guilt prompted extra petting and increased patience during his morning sniff circuit. Charlie loved me still.

And so it is with God. Each morning is filled with fresh mercies. He's teaching me each day to be better, a touch more like Him than the day prior. So often I fail. Yet in my worst moments, He loves me still. There's more than enough grace to cover our shame. He loves in such an extravagant way that I can't help but do and be better.

In my own efforts, I'm like Charlie. I devour things I shouldn't and tear apart other things. Before I met Jesus, I was a wreck. On days I don't stay close to Him, I'm not my best. He's taken all my worst parts, every sinful thing, and cast it into the sea. He remembers it no more. So, why should I? He sees me as clean and perfect, the righteousness of Christ. When He looks at me, and He does all the time, He sees Jesus because I'm covered by Him. He sees love and compassion. He sees right-standing, an adopted daughter. And that makes me level up! It makes me seek Him, spend time with Him, and learn about and talk to Him. It makes me want to shout to the world of His goodness! I am forgiven and you can be, too! I did nothing to earn forgiveness, except to believe in Him. I submit to Him daily, allowing Him to tweak my selfish parts, to realign lies I've believed, and to teach me truth. And in the process, I start to look more like Him. It's a grand transformation that starts with believing.

God forgives because He's paid the bill. He took the claim against us, the outstanding invoice, looked at the balance, and paid the bill in full. He now owns it, the one or many dark deeds are now covered by Him. Forgiveness is majestic and sublime. I don't see forgiveness often in humans; we prefer to hold onto our hurt, owning it like a prized possession or holding it over the heads of others. So proud of our personal garbage, we claim to be the thing we did or that was done to us. It's short-sighted and flat-out incorrect and, oh, how the enemy loves to keep us ineffective and invisible.

As a believer, God no longer sees that sin in us. We are forgiven. He doesn't side-eye or cross His arms in disgust. Much like Charlie, He is proud to be in our presence.

Points to Ponder

Do I identify as forgiven?

_____

_____

_____

_____

What would it take to claim full forgiveness?

_____

_____

_____

_____

Where do I need to forgive others?

_____

_____

_____

_____

What beliefs am I still carrying when He has covered all my sin?

_____

_____

_____

_____

19

LOOKING BACK

We all let Charlie out for potty time in different ways. Tim simply opens the door and stands alert on the front step to ensure Charlie doesn't bolt toward passersby. Maya and Cole drift from room to room, window to window, to determine his location and to ensure a walker or biker isn't rounding the curve. I prefer to apply the leash and walk him through the yard. I don't like the stress of wondering if someone is coming, I prefer the peace of a task completed quickly.

So, we walk the familiar ground, his potty territory, several times a day, which is never more than 5 feet away from an earlier visit. And with 99.9% of the visits, I have a strong desire to look at the damage. It's a strange curiosity that I hope I'm not alone in experiencing. I'm right there, it's nearly impossible not to look. A quick glance to see if some remnant of my digested underwear is peeking through, maybe to see how hydrated he is, maybe I'm even gauging the satisfaction of a successful poo? Either way, I look. Immediately feeling ridiculous, I turn and move in the opposite direction, always toward home. It's an impulse and then it's over. I never feel great about it, there's always something about looking back that's never satisfying.

There's something soothingly familiar about looking back, knowing what's visible, what's completed, what's known. What's behind us is the thing that seems most true. What I've experienced is oftentimes the only thing I know to be 100%. Good or bad, I can guarantee it happened. But lingering for too long in what lies behind robs me of the right now and delays my dreaming of what is to come. There'll never be another present moment, it flits by second by second, often unaware. There it is, the only April 22, 2020, at 6:40 and 30 seconds that will never be lived again. It's gone for good, already drifting behind. The trick is to stay here, and right here, again and again, planted in this exact moment. Looking behind at what's gone or anticipating what will be is pointless. So, over and over again, on circular repeat, I return to the present.

Where are my feet? Where are my thoughts? Am I noticing the lime green burst of buds popping from the trees where tomorrow's leaves will appear? Am I noticing the darkly wound purple irises ready to debut? Am I appreciating the splashes of uncapturable colors as the sun rises and sets? That specific sunset will never be that exact color pattern again, ever. It never was that exact color combination in all of history. It would be a shame to miss it. God has splashed the sky with light and colors and, so often, we scurry past His creation without even a glance.

I continually remind myself to be here, in the present, no looking back, no leaning forward. This lesson might be the most difficult to retain. There's comfort in looking back, I know what to expect, and I can place money on the past. But the present and future are completely unknown. I don't know what new stress or new celebration will present itself in the next five minutes or five years. I can only be here, now.

Even the being here is fleeting. There's another here now followed by another here now. New mercies every morning.

Lord, thank you for this breath, for this chair, for these thoughts. Thank you for this spring view, the swaying trees, and the birds announcing a new day. Thank you for clean water within arm's reach and a really good notebook to my right. This day has enough stress and enough joy to lean back or forward for too long.

His Word is filled with warnings on not looking back:

"No one who puts his hand to the plow and looks back is fit for the kingdom of God"
Luke 9:62

"But one thing I do: forgetting what lies behind and straining forward to what lies ahead"
Philippians 3:13

"Remember not the former things, nor consider the things of old. Behold, I am doing a new thing"
Isaiah 43: 18-19

Heck, He even turned Lots wife into a pillar of salt for looking back at the city He just decimated! (Genesis 19:26).

Lots of warnings (excuse the pun) to not turn around, to not look back. Look forward in eager anticipation. Trade your anxious thoughts for excitement. My past is filled with good and not-so-great moments. In each moment, there was something I learned, and full forgiveness when I completely missed the mark. In all of it, good and bad, it's building me to be the even better version I'm learning to be. There's no time to linger in the past, to dissect it from a safe perspective; the what-ifs and the wondering renders me ineffective, frozen.

So, do what you have to do, ask for or grant forgiveness, journal about it, and then throw it in the garbage; whatever it takes to put the past in the past. There's grace for it all, so take out the garbage, for there's good work to be done!

Points to Ponder

Where am I stuck in the past? What circumstance or event can I not move past?

_____

_____

_____

_____

_____

What happenings, hurts, wounds, unforgiveness, or mistakes occupy my thoughts? How can I reconcile these things so I can move forward into the present?

_____

_____

_____

_____

_____

Where do I need to be set free? In my emotions? In my grief? In my depression? In my addiction?

_____

_____

_____

_____

_____

Lisa Weigard

Have I asked God to set me free? Maybe today is a good day to start that conversation.

_____

_____

_____

_____

_____

20

HE KEEPS NO RECORD OF WRONGS

Tim and I eat out a lot. After a long day at work, when Charlie's best friend Tim returns home, we often leave him alone again for an hour-ish feast. Upon our return, oftentimes we'll pause at the basement door and listen for Charlie's howling. Charlie's howl is sad, lonely, and forlorn. His howl makes even the hardest of hearts melt and drop right into the tummy. Inching up the stairs, we try to catch him in full howl mode. I picture him seated, head up, neck craned to the ceiling like a wolf, but he always catches us rounding the corner. At that moment, just mere seconds from being so very sad, he's overjoyed to see us. Leaving his sad space, he greets us with tail wags and an underbite smile. Nothing is held against us, he doesn't pout the remainder of the evening, and our actions aren't held against us. The next hours before bed, he only wants to be beside us. He pulls his bed (often with our help) right beside us and rests, content once again. He simply wants to be near us.

If I rise for a drink, he watches. If I skip upstairs for a book or to check the laundry, he follows. His favorite place is right beside us, without any resentment. There were certainly days when I ignored him completely. Other days, so enmeshed in my work, I frustratingly rushed him and snipped at his needs. Again, he holds none of this against me. He reflects complete unconditional love. All wrongs are gone, no longer considered. He sees me only with love.

And so it is with God. Along my journey of walking with Him, I've charted my own path at times, going in directions not even close to His best for me. But when reason returned and I rounded the corner for home, He celebrated and welcomed me with open arms. He doesn't rub my nose in those errors. Instead, He removes each lie and wipes each tear away. Much like Charlie, God waits, expectantly watching the horizon for the outline of our return. And oh, how He celebrates that return. He crowns us, gives us a new identity, celebrates us with all the finest things, insisting on a Heavenly party. He even dances! Can you imagine God dancing because of you?

If I could compare Charlie's excitement at our return, I imagine God's eyes enlarging, his brows and shoulders lifting, the curve of his mouth turning up, and even His breath inhaling deeply in expectation. His feet scurrying forward, taking extra steps and hops to get closer to us sooner, His hands lifted and open as He heads toward us, lifting us in a twirly spin of joy! His Word says He'll never leave or forsake us, so He's with us in all our wandering. But oh, the joy at our return!

And once we're home, all our past wrongs are gone. Every awful thing, every selfish action is forgotten in God's loving gaze. He sees everything, even the inner workings of my heart and mind; yet He doesn't hold any of my wrongs against me. Never would I desire my innermost thoughts be broadcast for all to see, but to Him who knows them all, I'm as white as snow. The more I see as He sees, the less I want to do my own selfish things and the more I only want to seek out the things that bring Him joy!

Often my own short-sighted and selfish scurrying doesn't reflect His best plan, and some mild conviction is in order. Like a Good Father, He guides me in better thinking and better doing. There's no shame from Him. Conviction yes, shame no.

Much less these days, but in moments past, I would dredge from dark forgotten closets my most awful actions, trying them on for size. But they no longer fit. In fact, they stink. I'm not meant to wear those old clothes. That old baggage is no longer mine to carry. I think, surely these awful things are my identity. Nope. They aren't even part of my DNA. And if God doesn't consider them, if they are as far as the east is from the west, why do I insist on carrying or wearing them?

I am loved. I am in the process of being perfected. I am worthy. I am adopted into an unshakeable kingdom. Much like Charlie, God rejoices at our return and only wants to stay right beside us all our days.

Points to Ponder

Do I think God keeps a record of wrongs? Do I believe He has forgiven and forgotten my sins? Do I think I'm unworthy?

_____

_____

_____

_____

What would make me believe the truth?

_____

_____

_____

_____

Can I imagine Him dancing over me?

_____

_____

_____

_____

How can I begin to think as He does?

_____

_____

_____

_____

21

POO INTO PRAYERS

When we had a larger yard, we would let poo accumulate for a once-weekly scoop. Charlie tucked inside the house, always gazing longingly from the window, I'd wander the yard gathering poo before the lawn guy arrived. Oftentimes, I would find several deposits that weren't Charlie's. (A momma recognizes her children's work.) Charlie has definite size specifications, as a medium-sized dog deposits medium-sized mounds. These foreign invasive piles were small, teeny tiny droppings from a teeny tiny dog. Likely smelling Charlie's previous visits and wanting to add to the party, this trespassing tiny dog laid down its own contribution. I could go in a thousand directions here:

1. I should pick up all of Charlie's deposits right away. Yeah, I don't. I reserve that task for once a week.
2. Other people should pick up after themselves. Yes, they should, but they often don't.
3. People shouldn't assume it's okay to deposit more piles since there are already existing piles. Not cool.

I could work myself into a lather, email a few suspect neighbors, and order a big obnoxious sign of a dog squatting with a circle and slash through it and post it in my yard for all to see. But that wouldn't be very loving, would it? That wouldn't increase my peace, would it? That wouldn't teach my neighbors a lesson, would it? It surely wouldn't stop the droppings. I wouldn't be keeping the peace, and keeping the peace is more important than being right. Being right, I've learned, is a fleeting feeling. I prefer to be a peacekeeper, thankful for a strong back and moderate amounts of balance to bend and scoop, bend and scoop, a few times more. In the grand scheme of things, it's a 1" x ½" problem. I think I can handle that. What if it was a Great Dane-sized deposit? The bigger the poo, the bigger the annoyance? Suddenly, should a sizeable annoyance be worthy of losing peace? It's best just to bend and scoop.

I prefer my peace, I eagerly seek it, and this tiny deposit will not wreck my peace. So, in my bend and scoop, I say a little prayer for the owner of the trespasser. May they have peace, and may they have increased wisdom, stature, and favor. May their marriage be strengthened, their children be blessed, their income increase, and their hearts seek Him. I've suddenly increased peace on so many levels and my yard is poo-free! Feeling like a poo-prayer ninja, my unsuspecting neighbors are now receiving unexpected goodness from God.

Perhaps the poo is a 1" x ½" prayer card. Perhaps it's my own fragrant reminder of someone in need, someone that wouldn't have a friend to write a prayer request on their behalf. Couldn't every single thing be a reminder to pray? The ankle-bumping cart of the lady behind you in line, the last greedy grab of toilet paper, the car riding your bumper and flashing their lights, the family throwing an entire dinner of Popeye's garbage or a dirty diaper out the car window ... all lend the potential to pray. It's a split-second decision to make. Will it steal your peace, or will it inspire you to pray?

There's a distinct difference between healthy boundaries, not letting others walk on you, and protecting your peace. I'm not encouraging doormats here. There's no reason to be trodden upon, but my adult years have taught me which battles to fight, and poop is not one of them. Pick your battles, even better, place your battles in God's hands, pray it out, protect your peace, and move along.

So, plastic bag in hand and garden spade in another, I scoop and scoop some more. My yard, now clear for the lawn guy to safely travel without added squashing, is cleared of Charlie's droppings and the deposits of others. I've made the world a little better place, one scoop at a time. Meanwhile, I've made my own heavenly deposits, one with much sweeter fragrances.

Points to Ponder

What stresses me out?

_____

_____

_____

_____

Can I turn these stresses into prayer?

_____

_____

_____

_____

How can I pray for my neighbors?

_____

_____

_____

_____

How can I pray for my enemies?

_____

_____

_____

_____

22

MORE POO TALK

After a short yet sweaty walk, realizing it's both trash and lawn day, I decide to gather the poo early and be done with it. Plastic bag and scooper in hand, the hunt begins. Always searching for a good analogy and a distracting way to accomplish an unfun task, I parallel the ground poo to my own heart poo.

Search my heart, Lord, help me find the dark
places filled with anything but You.

Some piles are easy to find. Fresh piles still warm from the morning squat, sitting atop the grass. I remember where Charlie was that morning, so I head there first. Easier to remove, messy yes, but usually leaving no trace, with fresh air and grass now available to fill the spaces in between. No fear of stepping into that pile, but there are more, certainly.

The easy spots to recognize in my own heart are self-perpetrated … I'm my own worst critic.

Purge me of my pride, pluck away my need to please others,
take away anything in me that gets in the way of your work.

Rainy and busy days provided a weeklong gap between scoops, so surely landmines await. Careful steps as I quietly search for spots that don't belong. Spots not green, not thriving, indented where growth should be. Old piles have taken hold, gripping onto grass requiring more of a scrape than a scoop. Tugging at unwanted darkness, it wants to remain. It's familiar there, it's found a new home. These dark spots don't belong here and simply must go. So, like my phenomenal and detailed dental hygienist, I scrape and scrape until all hardness is gone. Picking and lifting, pulling and tugging till the grass, now clean, can grow in the right direction.

Old hurts, familiar yet unhealthy routines clogging my heart; some small, others bigger, taking up space in my heart that should otherwise be filled with Him. With Love. With Peace.

Show me, Lord, where the build-ups remain and scrape them away
with your gentle touch, leaving a clean space to be freshly filled.

The most annoying piles, though, are those left behind by others. Those unfamiliar deposits ... another dog has wandered onto the edges of our property and left unwanted treats. Keep your garbage to yourself, I think. Take care of your own issues and drama and darkness. It belongs neither in my yard nor in my heart. As if out of thin air ... not there yesterday, but still they appear.

Less than love-filled thoughts, comparisons, and complaints. Acting less than Godly, abusing the system, manipulating, and spewing untruths, adds chatter to my heart that should otherwise be occupied with love and hope for their future. Often starting small, like the tiny dog deposits, it quickly adds up over time. Taking space that should be occupied with Love, what remains instead is darkness, hardness, and bitterness. Love can't thrive in spaces filled with poo. The poo must be dug out and removed. More may arrive tomorrow and build up over the week, but a discipline must be created to search the yard and heart to lift it up before the grip begins.

Help me to love like you do, Lord. Protect me from evil and temptation.

*G*et in there and dig out that poo. It's a job only effectively completed by the owner with help from God. This task cannot be outsourced.

My now clean yard allows others to visit without worry. A barefoot walk in the grass, letting the cool strands slip between the toes and the dirt directly beneath grounds my otherwise busy circuits. A barefoot walk in a poo-filled yard is *no bueno*. Always looking for safe places to walk and the areas to avoid create a treacherous and stressful experience.

I've been around folks with poo-filled hearts and have had to navigate the land mines within … what to say, careful not to mention this or that, not digging too deep, not asking the necessary questions, staying surface level, avoiding that area, watching that step. It's exhausting. And draining. Unnecessary and off-plan. Get in there and dig out that poo. It's a job only effectively completed by the owner with help from God. This task cannot be outsourced.

Points to Ponder

Have I taken an in-depth look at myself lately?

_____

_____

_____

_____

If not, what am I afraid of finding?

_____

_____

_____

_____

What areas of my heart need cleansing? (Comparison, bitterness, fear, anger, doubt, shame...these are just a small sampling of heart poo.)

_____

_____

_____

_____

Ask Him to reveal the status of your heart. What areas does He suggest healing?

_____

_____

_____

_____

23

IMPATIENCE

My least favorite thing is taking Charlie for potty walks. He seems to sniff every single blade of grass (hear me when I say: every. single. blade.) along his leisurely stroll. At some tipping point, I grow impatient. I push and pull and verbally encourage him to drop his daily deposit, with no luck. I want the task list of items taken care of immediately, without delay, without the extra sniffs, without the extra leisure. No matter how hard I try, the pushing and pulling, the striving and struggling never seem to produce the desired results. It's only when I surrender and allow Charlie to relax and enjoy his investigative sniffs that the right things fall in line (excuse the pun). No matter how much I push and pull, redirect his steps, verbally redirect his focus, or encourage him to do the thing, he seems to know his own perfect timing, his own intricate dance, his own delicate balance of sniffs and strategic placement.

Me, however, I want all the things at this very moment. I don't wanna wait. Grant me full understanding, increased power, top-shelf wisdom, overflowing love, all the things. But it seems that the journey, the trust, and the building of a relationship are the secret sauce to all those important things, and so much more.

So, I exhale, drop my shoulders, settle back, and slow my roll. Without warning, my mental tendency to become Jo-Jo the circus monkey reappears, and the constant cycle begins again ... exhale, drop, settle, slow. Be here right now, seek the serenity, the fresh air on my skin, the grass beneath my feet, watching Charlie investigate all the little things I have overlooked. He perks to interpret the far-off call of another pup. Realizing it must have been simple gossip or needless chatter, he shrugs and returns to the sniff. Meanwhile, I exhale, drop, settle, slow yet again, and wait. The process can't be rushed.

Even as I reread this lesson for edits, yet again my mind has become Jo-Jo the circus monkey – thoughts jockey from which task to accomplish first. Does our church have strong intercessors? How are we to spiritually set captives free? Which car is a better transport for a shedding Charlie? Is there a need to cut Masonic ties from previous generations? How do I best pray for our country? And many other noises, some Godly, some simple distractions and fear-builders.

> *Be* still, don't strive, put down the cymbals, monkey-brain, and rest.

Stop and seek. Inhale and exhale. Where is God? What is He doing right now? What does He want me to do next? The best option for my brain is always to stop and seek. I desire to do, have, and be all that He died and rose to allow me to be, do, and have. I want to be at the finish line in everything and not in the middle of the race. I'm impatient. I must increase in trust – to know I'll be taught what I need for the moment. Trust that He has a better plan than I can even fathom and everything I need will be provided. I must also grow in discernment… that still small voice will tell me what I need to know and which direction I need to go, but the noise will distract me. I need to learn how to filter out the garbage to find that one crucial truth. Lastly, I must grow in obedience. Once I've gathered that one crucial truth instead of stashing it on the shelf, I must move forward boldly without delay.

It's conveniently easier to do all the other things instead of that one most important thing. Meanwhile, my impatience flares, perhaps because I'm not being obedient to the singular task, I should be doing in the first place. Impatience grows, I'm learning, when I neither trust, listen, nor obey. Impatience increases when I try to do everything in my own effort. There's a rush to get it done before the next distracting to-do arises. Be still, don't strive, put down the cymbals, monkey-brain, and rest.

Points to Ponder

When my impatience increases, am I trying to stop and practice learning to trust, listen, and obey God rather than trying to do everything in my own efforts?

_____

_____

_____

_____

What are my impatience triggers?

_____

_____

_____

_____

What helps me settle down when I'm triggered?

_____

_____

_____

_____

How can I grow in trusting more in the Lord?

_____

_____

_____

_____

24

PERSPECTIVE

Sometimes you have to do unfun things, like scrubbing the toilet or picking up poo, or walking your dog. Full transparency, I'd rather walk by myself, without any noise, without any stops or interruptions, so I can think and hear clearly. Today I learned that I must find the still small voice even during things I don't enjoy. Even in the middle of yuck, I must search out the yum. It's always there, it never leaves, I just muffle it with complaints, worry, and distraction. But even in those moments, God is there.

Training my heart to find Him despite myself and worldly distractions is the challenge, the adventure. No doubt life will get busier, more involved. The trick is to still my heart and mind even in the midst of busy, even in the midst of annoying tasks, to find where He stands and then do the same. Take that deep breath, close your eyes and with the imaginative portion of your heart and head, ask to see where He is and what He's doing. Is He seated? Is He standing? Is He noticing the beauty around Him? Is He in battle pose with sword drawn or seated and laughing, full of joy? If I was a gambling gal, I'd put money on the fact that He's right beside you, calm, not flustered, looking at you with that intense sparkly-eyed smile and saying you are very, very good. Now's a good time to waive the white flag and, staring back into those all-seeing eyes, hand over that heavy thought, and receive a better gift.

When I give in and take Charlie for a short walk, he pulls and sniffs and, in the break from life, I remind myself to breathe. In the sharp turn to the left, I train myself to say thank you for the shift in perspective … a new lawn to enjoy, a bird or butterfly I hadn't seen before.

Sometimes I get flustered when I've just gotten into the flow of work and Charlie interrupts for a potty break. Most times, it's just a curious sniff break he needs … no potty this time. My tendency when this happens is to yank him inside, toss down the leash, kick off my shoes, and sit back down to quickly reconnect to the flow. But when I slow down and shift my perspective, I see a butterfly. Then I feel the breeze. I wonder, has that flower always been so blue?

Wait, am I enjoying the fresh air? Sounds of the neighbor's water feature come into awareness, the soft sway of the birch tree. The chest tightness is slipping as deeper breaths are found. My toes release their grip, my tongue drops from the palate to the base, and my shoulders find gravity. Charlie is unaffected as he's always in the flow, always noticing, always aware, always appreciating. I, however, need constant reminders to look and see and smell.

One of many great mysteries is that God can be found in all things. He holds all things together so His very presence and character can be found in all things. The symmetry, the order, the intricate detail, nothing overlooked, nothing forgotten or not provided for, the multiplying cycle, the perfection. That truth makes me want to slow my roll and look closer. Even in the busy moments, even in the darkest places, especially in Walmart, there He is.

Where is He in that flower, where is He in the wind, where is He in this stillness? What does He want me to know right now? What joy am I discounting? Am I still enough to ask and listen or will I keep myself busy-minded and worry-filled and miss the message? The wild truth is there is no perfect situation to find Him. He's there always. It's me who is too busy. I layer on the extra tasks and allow unnecessary distractions. He says that whatever you do, do it with all your heart, as if working for the Lord and not for humans for it is the Lord you are serving. That shift in perspective makes folding the laundry, picking up the poo or taking Charlie on walks feel so very different.

Look around, find Him.

Points to Ponder

What is my typical perspective?

_____

_____

_____

_____

How can I consider a different perspective?

_____

_____

_____

_____

How can I find God in the unfun tasks?

_____

_____

_____

_____

When you imagine Him, what is He doing?

_____

_____

_____

_____

25

SUNNY SPOTS

On any sunny day, you can expect to find Charlie neatly tucked into something soft, directly within the confines of rays of sunshine beaming through the window. He appears so peaceful that I'm a tad jealous. I would love to have an adult-sized cushion that I could move from window to window, then just cast myself on it and rest in complete abandon. I'm not sure if I'm more jealous of the constant ability to nap, the soaking of the sun, or the reckless abandon he seems to be experiencing.

As the sun moves, Charlie moves strategically from ray to ray, always basking in the sunshine. All of it appears divine. At this moment, and then several more Charlie enjoys throughout the day, he's in such deep peace, surrendered, knowing all his needs and even a few desires will be taken care of. I know not all dogs experience this peace, and sadly not all receive the completion of their needs, but Charlie certainly does.

This makes me reflect on my own peace and surrender, or lack of it, each day. Every single day is fresh and new, yet some days, I flurry around without an ounce of the peace I have access to each moment. Instead, I'm task-driven, to-do list building, anxious for the limited amount of time I have in the day to reach full completion. And I'm certainly not tapping out all the surrender I'm capable of. I surrender an ounce of worry yet carry a ton. I desperately need to flip the script and, instead, surrender a ton and carry just an ounce. Perhaps one day when I reach full spiritual maturity, I will not even carry an ounce of worry.

All my needs are met by a good and gracious God who desires to give only good gifts to His children. He doesn't give snakes and rocks when we ask for bread and fish. He is Good. He created good because He is Good. So, why wouldn't we want to experience Him more and more all day long? Like Charlie, drifting from window to window, I should seek God in every moment. Not only reserved for Sundays, but I should also find that sunny spot and rest within His warmth. In fact, I should remember that I have become the sunny spot since He resides within. I no longer have to scurry around to find Him. God is right there beside me, even closer, nestled right in the folds of my gray matter, perched within the beating chambers of my heart.

That sun, that warmth, that peace, and that goodness, should radiate to every single person I pass. The lost, the prodigal, the wandering, the sad and defeated, the anxious, the blinded; they should all look upon us with sweet jealousy, wanting more of our secret sauce. Just like I look at Charlie on the soft cushion, basking in the warm sun, we should be so appealing to others that it draws them in, wanting to know God more. They should want to know Him by the way we walk, talk, and help; by the way we do business and serve others, and by the way we love.

We are called to be drastically different from the majority. Not better, but free. So, when they pass by and we are radiating that sweet surrender and we carry that peace that makes absolutely no sense in a world so chaotic and dark, that very presence within us should make them seek Him more. And then, more radiating sunny spots are present upon the Earth, spreading more Heaven here.

Oh, the potential for peaceful contagion! And yet, I often opt for the anxious scurry … flitting past the sunny reminders to rest, to cast my heavy burdens on His capable shoulders, thinking I can do better on my own, faster in my own efforts. Such worldly thinking, yet I permit and succumb to it over and over.

But today is a new day, filled with fresh mercies, and I have yet another good chance to rest, surrender and become a sunny spot.

Points to Ponder

What would it look like to be at complete peace?

_____

_____

_____

_____

Do I think I'm worthy of peace and presence? (Do you even realize that's an option?)

_____

_____

_____

_____

How important is it for me to radiate Him everywhere and in everything?

_____

_____

_____

_____

How can I radiate Him more?

_____

_____

_____

_____

26

PEACE

Charlie is my one unraveling. At complete peace coming straight out of my prayer room, filled to the brim with His presence, yet drained immediately from Charlie's needy whines for this or that. There my previously attained peace lays unused, tapped out, spilled all over the floor.

> *Go back to the Source. It's a constant refreshing!*

I can blame it all on Charlie; he needs something constantly. Yet, as I write, he's completely asleep, releasing soft snores on the bed beside me. I see him as one more thing I have to do, one more reason to sweep the floor, again and again, one more trip outside, one more of seemingly everything. Yet, it's not Charlie, it's me. My whining punches the hole that lets my peace spill onto the floor. My frustration is to blame. How can I jump so quickly from full to empty? Whining, frustration, annoyance, selfishness … they all instantly zap my peace.

It seems that maintaining peace is just as critical and necessary as finding it in the first place. It shows me how very weak I am on my own. There's no way I can walk in overflowing peace without His help. If I carried a bowl filled to the brim with water, I wouldn't rush, I'd walk carefully, with intention in each step. The same goes with peace, it seems. Always checking the level, do I need more? Has some spilled out? Go back to the Source. It's a constant refreshing.

Charlie will always need something: food, treats, a belly rub, or some sunshine for rest. It's my job to maintain my own peace while I'm helping meet his needs. In reality, he doesn't require a lot of assistance or attention, he's still sleeping, and his breathing has created a soothing in and out sound while I write. I make his needs bigger and wilder than reality all because I wanna do what I wanna do when I wanna do it. I don't want to be told to move here or there. I don't want to be interrupted when I'm in a good flow of cleaning or working.

The peace that comes from His presence is precious and should be handled with care. It's reassuring to know I always have more than enough peace available for any single thing. I simply need to touch base for a refill. But full transparency is that I don't touch base enough. I hustle and grind, running on fumes, then I wonder why I'm so short with Charlie; or worse, my two-legged family members. I didn't gather enough peace or, more truthfully, I let it spill out through worry or whining.

My all-time goal is to reach and remain in a full tank capacity of peace. Yet most days, I'm running with the low gas light on, gambling the distance till the next refill. Poor Charlie becomes the closest innocent victim to receive my frustration. Charlie becomes my mirror to reflect my current woeful state. In my interaction with him, I can easily gauge my peace level and, in most moments, it's far too low. So, return I must for a full refueling, moment by moment at times. Gauge, refill, gauge, refill. So, I sit and wait for God's presence. I turn on worship music, mentally searching for His presence (which is always nearby), and I acknowledge I can't do this alone. I need Him in every moment. I'm so sorry I ventured so far away from Him, I'm so sorry I whined, complained ... and I fill my mind, instead, with things of gratitude.

Thank you for your Presence, thank you that you're always with me,
thank you that you'll never leave or forsake me,
thank you that you have good plans for me.

Then I ask, what next? What next step should I take? Maybe just maybe, years from now, I'll be so spiritually mature that I can venture further without feeling so empty. Or perhaps spiritual maturity is knowing you never need to venture away from His Presence. My hope is that I can stay positioned right here, next to His side, never venturing solo ever again. So, now I just seek. I busily read over and did not apply the "Seek and you will find" scripture. So, I wait, exhale and inhale, mentally searching for His presence, like searching for your best friend at a party ... busy people everywhere but you can quickly spot your person from across the room by the sound of their voice, by the stature of their presence.

Sometimes my busy brain is too scurried, filtering through the thousand to-dos already plaguing my mind. But I'm equipped with the mind of Christ, so I can tell it what to do. The thousands of to-dos will wait (deposited promptly into a virtual basket by the door) and I wait. Sometimes I wait some more. It's me that's too busy, never Him. And there He is, patiently and kindly waiting. Once I've found Him, there's nowhere else I want to be, so I abide for a while. It's such a tasty place, I want more. Ready for all my questions, but also like a good friend, I wouldn't barrage them with a million wants, either. It's a communion ... a conversation, a push and pull, a give and take, a relationship. I give Him my worries, and search my mind, is there anything that's hindering my prayers, is there anything I'm holding back from Him?

Search my heart and mind, Lord.
Tell me how to draw even closer to you. How can I reflect you better?

I could do this life on my own, but I don't wanna. I've tried and it's just okay, simply mediocre. I want grand, I want bottomless joy, I want infectious love, I want abundant living, I want Him, every day.

Once I'm refilled, I walk carefully, attentively. Conscious of my words. Where am I whining? Where am I ungrateful? Both punch holes in peace like buckshot on a rusty tin can. Stay grateful. Stay expectant.

Regardless of what the world brings, regardless of the number of times Charlie taps his little toenails on the wood floor and stares with his beady eyes, I will nurture and protect my peace as if it's the most precious thing … because it is.

Points to Ponder

When was the last time I experienced God's peace? Do I access His peace every day?

_____

_____

_____

_____

How can I secure more peace in my day?

_____

_____

_____

_____

Am I often whining and complaining? (Stop it!)

_____

_____

_____

_____

Do I notice when His peace has departed?

_____

_____

_____

_____

27

AUTHORITY

As I've shared before, most mornings, I take Charlie on a sniff walk around the neighborhood. In typical fashion, we head across the street where the mailboxes clearly warrant numerous sniffs. Neighborhood dogs must leave messages galore for Charlie to decipher, interpret and translate.

Also, in typical fashion, I allow a specific amount of time for the sniff before I grow weary. One little tug is usually all that's required to get Charlie out of the depths and back on track. But this time the message must have been too good. He resisted, even pulled back. Knowing there were other areas to investigate, and my personal tasks were calling, I considered an allowance; a few more minutes of indulgence wouldn't damage anything, right? But no. We've indulged enough and now it's time to move on. There were other places to go and ultimately our own home to circle back towards. So, I pulled. I became the boss. I showed authority. And he moved.

Authority is a now fragile word. So many have abused it in attempts to tarnish its goodness. At one time, we had full authority, given to us by God, to name new creations, animals, and plants, and to subdue the earth (not of people, but of the enemy that prowled like a lion). We handed over our authority through disobedience and Jesus had to come and make things right again.

Fast forward to today. We've become lazy, complacent, distracted, and deceived. We've allowed the enemy to infiltrate every single important and powerful place. We surrendered our authority when we didn't speak up and when we assumed others shared our best interests. A few moments of indulgence have allowed deceptive influence to enter.

But no. Remembering it's not people to subdue but the enemy within, I'm recalling an old and powerful truth of our authority. Not by anything I did, only through Jesus who now lives in and through me, I have full authority to set things right once again.

Lord, open my eyes to the areas of authority that were once ours that now appear to belong to another.

- I reclaim our children from the grip of enemy influence.
- I reclaim our marriages from distortion and distraction.
- I reclaim our churches from the worldly desire to entertain and not offend.
- I reclaim our women from distraction and comparison.
- I reclaim my city and every city I've passed through back to the Lord. (What it sounds like … I claim this city for the Lord, in the name and by the blood of Jesus.)
- I reclaim our nation from division and fear.
- I reclaim our government from greed and corruption.

These words spill from my lips loudly as I circle my kitchen counter. These words land on the homes I pass on my walk, they saturate the streets I travel to my shop and back. I whisper them over my sleeping children, I shout them when I discover new areas of enemy occupation. I raise them to the sky, and I proclaim them to the ground.

Every enemy infiltration, from the highest places to the lowest, darkest area, is reclaimed with piercing authority. I may not occupy a place of worldly position, but my voice and my claims are heard in the heavenlies, and change happens.

One slight leash tug made all the difference that day. A new direction was gained, and a new perspective was found. Content no longer to sit and wait, I remembered my authority and I took a stand.

Points to Ponder

Do you realize you have authority?

_____

_____

_____

_____

What areas do I believe have shifted authority?

_____

_____

_____

_____

Where can I pull the leash and reclaim authority?

_____

_____

_____

_____

What areas in my life do I need to reclaim?

_____

_____

_____

_____

28

I'M THE BOSS

I almost created a monster. Here recently I've felt a restlessness in my spirit that can only be settled with a walk. A nice long solitary walk. Seems I go through seasons of stillness where it's perfectly adequate to pray while sitting or lying down. Then other times, I have to move.

Charlie took advantage of the movement and, from one considerate morning where I included him on a loop around the block, now every single time I rise and change into my workout clothes, he assumes it's all for him. Now he bounds down the steps, half floating, snorting much snot in his passive-aggressive ways of encouraging me to move faster to satisfy his needs.

Most days, he is a sleepy senior. But these mornings, he's a sugar amped temperamental toddler. I lead him into the garage and, while I lace up my sneaks, he snorts snot everywhere. I care mildly less since the milky goo lands on the concrete floor, but the sound certainly grates my soul. My shoes take time ... they're sock-like and take sweet time or else my actual socks will sneak down into my shoe causing an uncomfortable annoyance.

I like to take my time; I don't like to be rushed. I like to savor the feel of my socks. I want to appreciate the agility of my hands to create loops on the laces. My desire is to savor every single thing. But his highness awaits. Already I'm annoyed.

I loop on his leash and off we go. He's clearly excited, but I am not. Much like having a party and that annoying uninvited guest appears, I tolerate Charlie but I'm not joyful. And off we go ... my personal loop is much longer. I typically lead Charlie only around the horseshoe drive of our court. But even that loop seems too long. Some days I simply take him for a 100-yard half-court hike. It's the leisurely jaunt of a thousand sniffs. There's no exercise for me and certainly not often the peace that comes with a good solid undistracted prayer walk. In addition, I'm not the sweetest of dog moms at this moment ... this is supposed to be my time, and Charlie has jockeyed in on my walk. I wait patiently for approximately 50 grass and bush and electric box sniffs, but around 51 I'm done. Frustration abounds, eye rolls begin, and short sniffs of annoyance are flared. In this aspect, I'm not much different than Charlie ... we both sniff and snort our frustration in hopes of increasing the pace. (Perhaps we're both passive-aggressive ... that's for another day). I direct the leash towards home, refusing those last million sniffs.

One morning, I heard God's voice whisper, *"I never told you to take him along."* Ouch. Sometimes even the nicest of gestures are only a distraction or procrastination. My time with Him is just that ... my time with Him. I must set that time apart as holy, letting nothing come against it. And come against it, it does! But God reminded me that I'm the boss ... not the same as God being the boss, of course, but I have the authority to say no. I have the authority to change the routine. I am perfectly capable of saying, "Not today," or "I'll take you later, this is my time." I even have the authority to say nothing at all and still do the thing God has instructed me to do, without excuse or explanation.

This revelation was so liberating, creating a shift between being reactive and proactive, between being tossed about like waves on the ocean and standing on solid ground. Big difference. I have the power to make the time precious. I have the authority to say no.

I always feel such liberation when I finally return Charlie to the house and turn around for my own personal walk. I like Charlie, most times I even love him, but he's not the boss of me. I only have one Boss. And He loves spending time with me. He quiets my soul, He gives me direction, He tames the busy brain, He's my medicine. With all those benefits, I should allow nothing to come against this precious time together. Not even my four-legged family member.

God whispered authority to me that day which I'm glad to activate. I will not leave that authority on the shelf to gather dust, assuming the noisy world has a greater claim on my time and mind. So tomorrow, sweet Charlie, you'll have to watch me gear up, glide down the stairs, and walk straight out the door without you.

Points to Ponder

Where have I dismissed my authority to other things?

_____

_____

_____

_____

What areas of authority can I reclaim?

_____

_____

_____

_____

Do I spend time with God every single day?

_____

_____

_____

_____

What excuses have I allowed instead of solo time with Him?

_____

_____

_____

_____

29

TO HIM, I AM EVERYTHING

To Charlie, I am everything. I am the food source, the walk giver, the poop scooper, the water filler, and the ear scratcher. Charlie depends on me to accomplish the daily tasks, and anything extra is golden. Of course, if I don't participate, someone else will surely be chosen to fulfill the daily task and receive the daily reward (or nightly snuggle). But he likes it when I work with him. He appreciates my assistance. Even when I don't want to, even when I'm feeling overwhelmed, time with Charlie never disappoints. He continues to teach me new things, reveal my own weaknesses, and point me to God.

I'm crazy proud of the light I carry. God's presence within me can light up the darkest of places. Some days, however, the worldly darkness is just too much, and it would be so much easier to stay in bed, pulling the covers over my eyes and hiding. Like today. In a leisurely social media scroll, the revelation of a specific evil was exposed. You could certainly insert any evil here; the choices are endless these days.

Today's evil involved the most vulnerable: unborn babies. Things that are graphic and painful to hear, but necessary to know. This information pierces my sunshine and rainbow bubbled heart. How could these things happen? What purpose did these things accomplish? What gain have we possessed by these deeds done in darkness? How are we not aware? How can we remain silent while such evil is happening?

My spiraling mind is overwhelmed. What could this one quiet, boutique owner possibly do to make a change? How could anyone even consider moving this mountain? It's too dark, it's too deep. And then I hear His small voice…

"Use what you have in front of you.
Use the gifts you already have."

> **And this mountain will surely move into the sea.**

Being a big believer in prayer, I figured that was a good start. Praying immediately was the first step. And I have a good hour before the shop opens each Friday and a wide-open deck on which to gather, so let that be step two. Mountains (aka, high places of lower case 'g' gods) will move with the faith-filled words of His people. Darkness is revealed in the light of His presence. In fact, darkness itself becomes light once exposed. So, let that be my contribution to the fight. Even if it's just my voice on the deck each Friday, God is pleased and will send out angel armies to enforce and enact the requests. So pray, I will. The harvesting and gathering, the income, the trafficking and distribution, the research, the transport, the stacking and counting, the disassembling, and the disposal will all be covered in my sword-filled words. And this mountain will surely move into the sea.

Over and over in the scripture, situations get really, really bad. Dark things happen. Faith and hope seem like they might never be restored. And always, a God-loving human steps up while God shows up. For every evil, there are two little words that always let me know the tide is changing: But God. This world seems to be darkening daily and too often things seem far beyond repair, but God. Corruption has deep roots and far-reaching tentacles, but God. Our wee ones are so vulnerable, but God.

My frame and influence might be small, but my voice and my faith are giants to Him. To Him, I am everything.

Points to Ponder

What topics seem too big for me to tackle alone?

_____

_____

_____

_____

Do I know how big God is?

_____

_____

_____

_____

How can I tackle my mountain today?

_____

_____

_____

_____

What resource is right in front of me? What special skill do I have to use? (Use these!)

_____

_____

_____

_____

30

SEEING UNSEEN THINGS

On quiet nights and lazy afternoons in years past, I would spy Charlie staring at some particularly ordinary corner of my bedroom. One time I watched him rise from his typical snuggled slumber to crisp alert and let out a low, deep growl. He wouldn't lay down, he wouldn't move, something had unnerved him. Something unseen. He's not a particularly nervous dog and doesn't become agitated on most days, so this behavior really struck me as unusual. In a typical human response, I followed his gaze to determine the reason for his alarm. Seeing nothing, I encouraged him to return to rest and, only after a long dialogue of calm words, he returned to my side, remaining on watch.

On other days he'd awake from deep sleep to wander around the bedroom, unsettled. He'd pace to one corner then another, unsure. He'd hide under my desk, cowering. These strange behaviors piqued my curiosity. I do believe dogs (and children) can see things our adult minds have long ago reasoned out of awareness. What things are out there, how did they get in, and how do I usher them away? Charlie, once again, pointed me in the direction of God.

Lisa Weigard

Dusting off my Bible, I began to read, "Stronger is He who is in me than he who is in this world." God's Word and His name are our weapons. But much like the first time I fired a rifle, if I'm untrained and unaware, the weapon isn't nearly as effective. So, the study began. I began to learn about our authority. I wrote out scripture and set it to memory. I played and sang worship music more often. All that was a good and elementary start. The meatiest weapon was gained when I spent time with God. In hushed tones, He told me what He thinks of me. He helped me discern truth from a lie. He changed my desires to align with His desires. Anything less felt awkward and unwelcome.

Scripture tells the story of a priest who was attempting to rebuke demons. The demons themselves were aware of the apostle Paul and Jesus, but they were not familiar with the priest (Acts 19:14-16). This priest had no relationship with Jesus, just copycat verbiage, and what resulted was a "darkness winning throwdown." The priest, well versed in scripture and worship and rituals, carried no authority because he didn't know Jesus. He hadn't spent time in His presence, he hadn't asked questions and listened for answers. He hadn't created a friendship.

I've had the honor of ushering demons from a tormented soul. I didn't see it coming and the strength was not my own. My role was a neutral but loving and willing conduit between heaven and earth. I was in the right place at the right time, and I leaned fully on Him and the relationship we had created together.

Seeing this reminded me that there are indeed things we're not aware of, things that haunt and torment, that linger in dark corners waiting for the opportunity to pounce. This experience made me level up my prayers over my children, my husband, my home, business, and friends … nothing has been off-limits in my prayers. But the even better result was the awareness

138

of my dire need for God. It made me want to know Him more, to seek Him out, fight diligently against all distractions, listen to Him, learn about Him, and sit quietly and chat with Him.

I needed to know the One strong enough to pluck the darkness out of a human that day. That decision ranks highest on my best decisions list. It's one that I'll never regret or forget, for sure. And it's just the beginning of a long and loving relationship with Him.

Charlie rarely rises in response to unseen things anymore. My house is covered, and my sleep is sound.

Points to Ponder

Do I ever sense unseen things?

_____

_____

_____

_____

Do I know the Power to rid demons?

_____

_____

_____

_____

Have I spent time with God in friendship?

_____

_____

_____

_____

How can I get to know Him better right now?

_____

_____

_____

_____

31

REAL JOY

Joy is so much more than happiness. It's trusted contentment and Charlie has it in spades. He trusts that once I finish brushing my teeth and washing my face, I'll climb into bed, and he will jump up for his nightly snuggle. He appreciates my random ear itching and leans into Tim's hugs. His wagging tail indicates his inner happiness during Grandma visits. He doesn't fake his joy, it comes naturally. He doesn't turn his joy on and off; the potential is always there and it's always authentic. He doesn't fabricate a more joy-filled appearance. If he isn't joy-filled, he's content to rest until the opportunity rises once again. Charlie truly has so much to teach his two-legged mom.

Very recently, I wondered why I was always so tired. I investigated my eating habits and made modifications with slight improvement. I increased my workouts (full transparency: after over a year of no workouts, I simply started moving) and noticed some toning. I reduced my alcohol intake to consume (mostly) only on days beginning with S's. And still, I felt drained.

Everything in my life was good, I just felt meh about everything. In this current world climate, nearly every single human is feeling meh. Maybe more than meh. I can imagine most feel fearful, depressed, drained, angry, suspicious, and perhaps even hateful. So being exhausted seemed normal.

Everything necessary was being completed, I just couldn't put my finger on what was wrong or missing. In fact, I didn't even detect anything was wrong at all. I never said anything to a single soul. I was just pressing through and doing all my normal things with not as much joy. Truly, I had no joy and didn't even know I was missing it. Instead, I had fabricated what I thought was joy and pasted it all over myself. This must be what being a joy-filled Christian looks like, so I built an image of joy instead of seeking it out in God. But I'm getting ahead of myself.

I run with a group of top-notch prophetic sisters and, on a regularly scheduled gathering, my name was whispered in their hearts. Turns out, God knew why I was so tired, and He loves me enough to make it right. My heart had become rock hard through comparison, performance, disappointment, and lack of trust. My blood beating heart had become a crystalline block of blackened obsidian. From the outside, I appeared smiley but had no fruit to share or roots to withstand heavy winds. I truly had no idea … my days were filled to the brim with routine busyness and not enough time with Him. I was exhausted and couldn't find the source. I went to church on Sunday but left feeling no different. The Word had not pierced my heart. I hadn't worshipped in Spirit and in Truth. I lifted my hands but didn't fully let Him in. I read my Bible and a daily devotional but hadn't allowed enough time to simply listen for His voice. Truly, I hadn't even asked him a question. If I had asked about the state of my heart, I might have gained insight and remedy, but I plugged along with fabricated joy pasted on my face not even knowing there was an easier and fully authentic source so nearby. I knew all the right things to say but wasn't letting them creep into my own hardened heart. My head was filled with knowledge, but it hadn't traveled the long 12" down to my heart. The days after that insightful gathering will occupy an entire book (perhaps book #2) but for now, know my heart has been softened through surrender, His joy now perches upon my person, and I want nothing less than fully authentic Joy.

By comparison, I now see that the joy available to us is so much better even than Charlie's version. His isn't rooted in knowing and trusting Jesus. This Godly version of joy is so much more than a tail-wagging response to a treat. It's so much more than a lit-up face when his favorite grandma arrives. It's so much more than belly rubs and nightly snuggles. It's the contentment that comes when someone knows all the good things and all the bad things but loves me fully and sees me as perfected. Right now. Not after this book is published, not just when I attend church, not more on a good day and less on a bad day.

This joy comes from sitting with God and reading His love note in His very near company, asking Him questions about it, and agreeing it's for me. These days, I smile a little less but only because the fabricated smile I carried forever was too big and exhausting ... now my smile is real, authentic, and based on Him. But even more than a smile, the joy that comes from time with Him sustains me in tough times. It reminds me of my early dating days with Tim, getting off the phone after hearing his voice and feeling all warm and fuzzy for hours ... practically hovering around my apartment wondering when I'd talk to him again.

Joy is a by-product of spending time with God. It's a natural fruit created in friendship. I've learned the hard way that performing joy is futile, ridiculous, and draining. If you wonder if the joy you're experiencing daily is from Him or whether, like me, you've built your own version, spend some time with Him. Ask Him. I can provide a five-star, 100% satisfaction guaranteed review of knowing Him ... it's always good and He's not done with me yet.

Points to Ponder

On a scale of 1 to 10, with 1 being the least, what is your measure of joy?

_____

_____

_____

_____

_____

Ask the Lord how to increase joy in your life and commit to meet with Him to bring about this change.

_____

_____

_____

_____

_____

Throughout this book, you have journaled about distractions and been challenged to give Him your undivided attention during your day. Have you seen the joy in your life increase because of this practice?

_____

_____

_____

_____

_____

Spend some time with Him. Read scriptures that talk about joy. Journal them below. Add your thoughts.

_____

_____

_____

_____

_____

Lisa Weigard

A FINAL WORD
HE'S DESPERATE TO REACH US

Throughout Scripture, God uses animals to reach people. He'll use nearly any single thing to snag our attention, in fact. I mean, He did create it all, so why shouldn't He use it to capture our eye? I remember reading about:

The talking donkey, saving his rider from an angry angel,
>a fish carrying abundant tax payments,
>>a ginormous fish swallowing a disobedient Jonah, and
>>>bears charging from the forest to deliver vengeance for Elisha.

God is still working on increasing my patience as I still want everything done quickly. Lord, teach me, help me remember to apply it, then let's move on to the next lesson.

God uses every single thing to draw us closer to Himself. So, why shouldn't He use Charlie with his fearsome appearing underbite and endless shedding of hair to teach me more about His very character? The trick is slowing down enough to notice. Over time, I grew so used to learning some new thing from Charlie that I became expectant for the next small lesson.

What do you have to teach me today, Lord, through Charlie?

Lisa Weigard

Charlie isn't perfect. Neither am I. But every day, God finds creative ways to teach me new things about Himself, what He thinks about me, and ways to be more like Him. Some lessons take a few repetitions to settle in. I wish I learned things more quickly, but it seems I'm rather stubborn.

But God, much like Charlie, is very patient; certainly, more patient than me. But then again, He's the Creator and Source of patience. If anyone should be patient it would be Him. So, He waits without annoyance until I finally get it, apply it, and allow it to change me from the inside. There's no better teacher than the One who created it all. So, I wait, with expectant eyes and an open mind for the next lesson. He's still working on increasing my patience as I still want everything done quickly. Teach me, Lord, help me remember to apply it, then let's move on to the next lesson.

It seems I even rush the learning. I certainly rush Charlie through his slow sniffing of every blade of grass, eager to get back inside so I can tackle the next to-do. When in fact, I, too, should be inhaling and exhaling, enjoying, and savoring.

So often, though, I claim to know best. My way is the best way, or my pace is the best pace. Wanting it all, I began to eagerly devour His Word or listen to sermons, waiting for the next a-ha moment. What's on the menu? What wisdom is available to me? Instead of waiting for Him, I frantically search for knowledge in every place except in Him. Sifting the sermons for some small parcel, some nugget of knowledge, I too soon find myself frustrated and ineffective.

Seemingly at snail's pace, His lessons through Charlie began to settle and pointed me in a new direction, going direct to the Source. No longer eager for the next lesson through Charlie, I wanted the lesson direct from Him,

148

which is the exact place He wanted me to be all along. He's patient and eager to have us close by.

My suggestion? Skip the scurry and go directly to the Source. Ask Him: What's next? What do you want me to know about this situation? Balance it out in His Word to be sure it's God and not some similar-sounding voice. Be patient (still working on that one) and keep those eyes open. He may use a favorite pet, a worship song, an unexpected and encouraging word from a friend, a spectacular sunset … all of it points back to Him if we only take notice. All creation sings to Him, even the rocks could cry out to Him, so how then should His crowning creation, His most favorite sons and daughters, react to Him? I get it … we've been trained to be self-sufficient, strong, and believe only the things we see right in front of our eyes. But there's so much more.

If you don't know how to find Him, pick up your Bible. He's there. If you don't think He sees you, worship, He's with you, He sees you and He adores everything about you. If you don't think He'd like what He sees, if you think you're too bad, too rotten, too ugly, too dark, then you aren't looking closely enough at the cross. He saw the grand divide that sin created between a most Holy God and our sin covered self, and He left His throne for you, climbed up on a cross for you, died for you, entered Hell for you; He defeated the enemy for you, made a public spectacle of the enemy and all the lower case g gods for you, hung around to eat, heal and teach, then gave us back the authority that had been stolen; and He sits, fully alive right beside our most Holy Father, still interceding for you, until He comes back and silences the enemy once and for all, for you. It's scandalous and overwhelming if you take the moments it deserves to really ponder and believe.

More than anything, He desires and deserves your love and wants only to pour out buckets and buckets of love upon you. Will you take a moment to be still and receive?

Points to Ponder

Why have I been procrastinating spending time with Him? Am I trying to learn from sources other than Him?

_____

_____

_____

_____

What personal weaknesses do I need His help with?

_____

_____

_____

_____

I've heard Him knocking. Why don't I open the door and let Him in?

_____

_____

_____

_____

Where can I find Him today?

_____

_____

_____

_____

SPECIAL THANKS

I am most grateful for my husband, Tim who supports, encourages, and loves me daily. I'm lovingly grateful to Maya and Cole and their willingness to listen as new revelations appeared even before words had yet to curl around concepts.

I am thankful for supportive friends who spoke life against my procrastination and doubt:

> Cara Achterberg (writer and dog lover),
> Jen Bonitz (fellow reader and stellar friend),
> Kristy Thompson (fierce encourager and love seeker),

I am thankful for my Jesus girls:

> Krystal Woods (trailblazing scripture teacher and Presence bringer),
> Jen Mattheu (top-notch discerner and truth speaker),
> Christina Taylor (people-pleasing discarder and gentle giant),
> Kim Bonvissuto (worship warrior and God seeker).

Thank you to Nancy Slattery whose photos captured Charlie so perfectly … the treats in your pocket didn't hurt, either.

Thank you to Kelly Willie, fellow writer, and Jesus-girl, whose gentle spirit and deep desire to seek and carry His Presence inspires me.

Lisa Weigard

Kelly introduced me to Mary Ethel Eckard who massaged this collection of thoughts into something understandable. Thank you, Mary, for using your skills to make this book a reality.

And always, I thank God for being so very patient with me. Your daily whispers to write were ignored and for that I'm sorry. You always know best.

ABOUT THE AUTHOR

Lisa Weigard owns Soulshine Boutique, an adorable women's clothing store in Shrewsbury, Pennsylvania. One might even say it's her favorite place of reflecting God and ministering to the hearts of women through sharing encouragement, prayer, and the love of Christ. She loves bougie chocolate and all things peanut butter, and she recharges alone, preferably with a cup of excellent loose-leaf tea. Lisa and her husband, Tim, live in York, Pennsylvania with their daughter Maya, son Cole, and their dog, Charlie.

You can contact her at CharlieMeThee@gmail.com.

Made in the USA
Middletown, DE
28 July 2022

CHARLIE, ME, *and* THEE

Things My Dog Taught Me About God

A must-read for dog owners
How a beloved pup can point us toward God
Gather wisdom and life lessons from a dog and his owner

Meet Charlie, a puggle pup, (a mix of pug and beagle), and his owner, Lisa, a boutique owner, wife, and mom, who rescued and adopted him. Little did she know, Charlie had a little rescuing of his own to do. Within the pages of this book, the author shares how God used a puggle pup named Charlie to teach her about herself, others, and Him. Life with Charlie caused her to slow down, look around, and ponder life, family, worry, and work. These tiny glimmers of light pointed her to one source – God. She articulately and transparently shares the lessons learned and encourages the reader, through questions at the end of each day, to personally ponder the insights. Her words give insight into how a loving and loyal pet can teach us how to pause, ask, listen, seek, awaken, own, obey, rest, and savor life. And who doesn't want more of that! This is a 31-day devotional designed to help you in your daily walk with God. Take these revelations and make them your own. Apply them to your life, family, and thoughts. And don't be surprised when you awaken to a deeper and more meaningful relationship with the Maker of your very soul.

LISA WEIGARD owns Soulshine Boutique, an adorable women's clothing store in Shrewsbury, Pennsylvania, and also her favorite place of reflecting God and ministering to the hearts of women. Lisa and her husband, Tim, live in York, Pennsylvania with their daughter Maya, son Cole, and their dog, Charlie.

$15.00
ISBN 979-8-9857287-3-6
51500>
9 798985 728736

Mary Ethel